White Rose MATHS

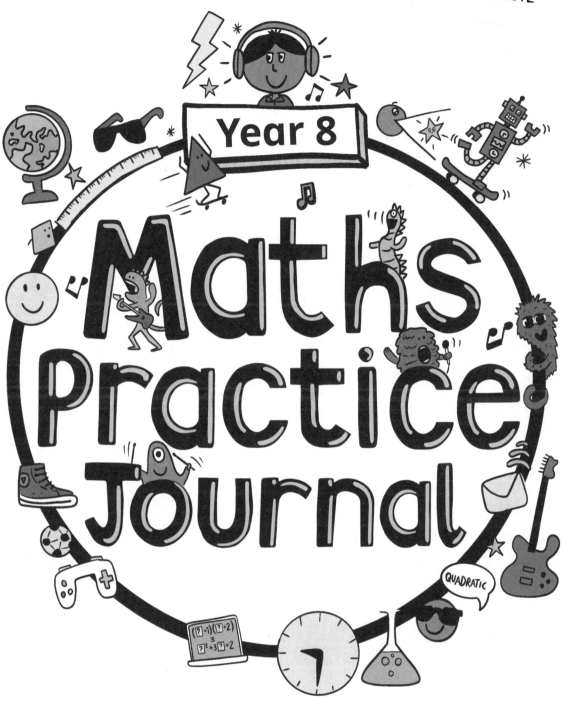

Year 8

Maths Practice Journal

Author: Emily Fox

Series Editor: MK Connolly

OXFORD
UNIVERSITY PRESS

Contents

Block 1 Ratio & scale

In this block, you learn about **ratio** – that is a way of comparing two or more quantities. This **bar model** shows us that there are 2 adults for every 7 children on a school trip. You can write the ratio of adults to children as 2:7

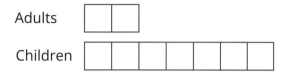

You can use bar models to help you solve problems with ratio. If Mo shares 42 sweets with Whitney in the ratio 2:5, that means Whitney will be getting a lot more sweets than Mo! Maybe you can see how many more?

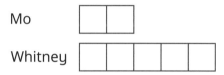

You learn to write ratios in their simplest form. In its simplest form, the ratio of yellow (Y) to green (G) squares is 3:2. Can you see why?

G	G	Y	Y	Y
G	G	Y	Y	Y

You also write ratios in the form 1:n. That is very useful because it is like saying for every 1 of these there are n of those. In this triangle, the ratio of base to height is 2:4, which is the same as 1:2

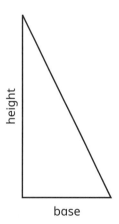

Key vocabulary

Ratio   Bar model   Simplest form   Simplify   Proportion

Equal parts   Share   Scale   Units

Ratio & scale

Date:

Let's remember

1   List the factors of 20 _____

2   Write the first six multiples of 15 _____

3   List the prime numbers between 10 and 20

_____

4   Solve $x + 19 = 37$ $x =$ ☐

Let's practise

1   Complete the sentences to describe the red (R) and blue (B) counters.

   a) For every 4 red counters, there are ☐ blue counters.

   b) For every ☐ blue counters, there are ☐ red counters.

   c) The ratio of red to blue counters is ☐ : ☐

   d) The ratio of blue to red counters is ☐ : ☐

2   Complete the sentences to describe the shapes.

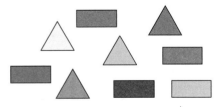

   a) For every ☐ triangles, there are ☐ rectangles.

   b) The ratio of triangles to rectangles is ☐ : ☐

   c) The ratio of rectangles to triangles is ☐ : ☐

3   A vase has pink, yellow and white flowers.
    The ratio of pink to yellow to white flowers is 2:7:5

    Write the ratio of

    a) pink to white flowers ☐ : ☐

    b) yellow to pink flowers ☐ : ☐

    c) white to yellow flowers ☐ : ☐

4   $a = 8, b = 3, c = 7$

    Complete the sentences.

    a) The ratio of a to c is ☐ : ☐

    b) The ratio of b to a is ☐ : ☐

    c) The ratio of c to a is ☐ : ☐

5   Pink paint is made using red paint and white paint in the ratio 1:3

    Red ☐

    White ☐☐☐

    a) How much pink paint can be made using 6 litres of red paint?

        ☐ litres

    b) How much pink paint can be made using 6 litres of white paint?

        ☐ litres

6   Dora and Ron share some money in the ratio 1:5

    a) If Dora gets £30, how much money does Ron get?

        £ ☐

    b) If Ron gets £30, how much money does Dora get?

        £ ☐

7   On a school trip, there must be 2 adults for every 7 children.

Adults

Children

There are 35 children going on the school trip.

How many adults must go on the trip?

8   A shop orders apples and bananas in the ratio $8:5$

a) If there are 80 bananas, how many apples are there?

b) If there are 80 apples, how many more apples than bananas are there?

9   Mo and Whitney share 42 sweets in the ratio $2:5$

Mo

Whitney

How many more sweets does Whitney receive than Mo?

10   $a:b:c = 3:2:7$

$a + b + c = 480$

Work out the value of c.

$c =$

How did you find these questions?

| Very easy | 1 | 2 | 3 | 4 | 5 | 6 | 7 | 8 | 9 | 10 | Very difficult |

Ratio & scale

Date:

Let's remember

1   For every 7 blue counters in a box there are 3 red counters.

   What is the ratio of blue to red counters?   ☐ : ☐

2   Find the lowest common multiple of 8 and 6   ☐

3   What is the probability of getting tails when you flip a fair coin? _____

4   What is the size of each angle in an equilateral triangle?   ☐°

Let's practise

1   Write the ratio of blue (B) to red (R) squares in its simplest form.   ☐ : ☐

B	B	B	R	R
B	B	B	R	R
B	B	B	R	R
B	B	B	R	R

2   Write each ratio in its simplest form.

   a) 3 : 12 = ☐ : ☐   c) 48 : 40 = ☐ : ☐

   b) 16 : 12 = ☐ : ☐   d) 35 : 56 : 21 = ☐ : ☐ : ☐

3

   a) What fraction of the bar is striped? $\frac{☐}{☐}$

   b) Write the ratio of striped to plain.   ☐ : ☐

4   In an animal sanctuary, the ratio of dogs to cats is 2 : 3

   a) What fraction of the animals are cats? $\frac{☐}{☐}$

   b) $\frac{2}{7}$ of the dogs are female.

   Write the ratio of female dogs to male dogs.   ☐ : ☐

5   A box contains white, milk and dark chocolates.

$\frac{3}{20}$ of the chocolates are dark. $\frac{2}{5}$ of the chocolates are milk.

Write the ratio of white to milk to dark chocolates. ☐ : ☐ : ☐

6   Simplify the ratios.

a) 40p : £1 = _____

b) 5 kg : 400 g = _____

c) 30 minutes : 3 hours = _____

7   Here are some yellow (Y) and green (G) squares.

a) i)   For every 4 yellow squares, there are ☐ green squares.

ii) For every 2 yellow squares, there are ☐ green squares.

iii) For every 1 yellow square, there are ☐ green squares.

b) Write the ratio of green to yellow squares in its simplest form. ☐ : ☐

8   Write these ratios in the form $1:n$

H

a) 4 : 12 = _____

b) 2 : 7 = _____

c) 4 : 5 = _____

d) 12 : 6 = _____

9   a) The ratio of base : height is ☐ : ☐

H

b) Write this ratio in the form $1:n$ ☐ : ☐

c) What is the gradient of the unknown side? ☐

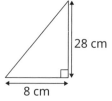

28 cm

8 cm

10 Simplify the ratio

$18y^2 : 54y$ = ☐ : ☐

How did you find these questions?

Very easy   1   2   3   4   5   6   7   8   9   10   Very difficult

8

Block 2 Multiplicative change

In this block, you move on from ratio to start learning about **direct proportion** – that is where you have two quantities, and as one increases the other one also increases at the same **rate**. You can use a table to show direct proportion relationships, like this one.

Time (s)	10	20	30	40
Distance (m)	11	22	33	44

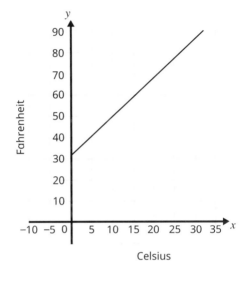

You also use graphs to represent direct proportion relationships, like this **conversion graph** that shows the conversion of temperature from degrees Celsius to degrees Fahrenheit.

You will find out about the **scale factor** that links two **similar shapes**. These two triangles are similar, and the scale factor from the smaller triangle to the larger one is 3.5

Can you see how to work that out?

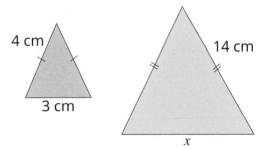

You will also explore **map** scales. Have you seen maps where it says it is drawn to a **scale** of 1:50000? That means every 1 unit of length on the map represents 50000 units in real life.

Key vocabulary

Direct proportion   Conversion graph   Scale factor   Rate

Similar shapes   Map   Scale   Linear

Multiplicative change

Date:

Let's remember

1   The ratio of triangles to circles is 3 : 5

What fraction of the shapes are triangles?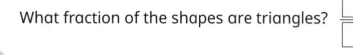

2   For every 5 students, there is 1 teacher.

If there are 30 teachers, how many students are there?

3   List the factors of 30 _____

4   $\dfrac{1}{4} + \dfrac{1}{3} = \dfrac{\square}{\square}$

Let's practise

1   Cupcakes are sold in boxes. Each box contains 8 cupcakes.

   a) i)   How many cupcakes are there in 2 boxes?

     ii) How many cupcakes are there in 7 boxes?

   b) Chocolates are also sold in boxes. Each box contains 30 chocolates.

     i)   How many chocolates are there in 5 boxes?

     ii) How many chocolates are there in 50 boxes?

     iii) How many boxes would you need to buy to have more than 5500 chocolates?

2   Oil is sold barrels. 5 barrels of oil costs £400

   a) How much do 50 barrels of oil cost?

   b) How much do 35 barrels of oil cost?

   c) How much do 2 barrels of oil cost?

3   The graph shows the approximate conversion between kilograms (kg) and pounds (lb).

a) Use the graph to make approximate conversions.

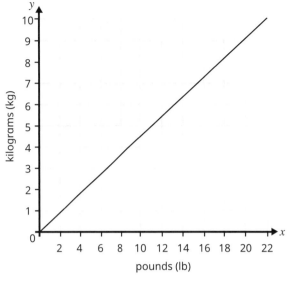

i)   10 kilograms ≈ ☐ pounds

ii) 4 kilograms ≈ ☐ pounds

iii) 10 pounds ≈ ☐ kilograms

iv) 18 pounds ≈ ☐ kilograms

b) Use the graph to make an approximate conversion of 70 kilograms to pounds.

☐ pounds

4   The currency in Dubai is the UAE dirham (AED).   1 AED = £0.22

a) Complete the conversions.

i)   10 AED = £ ☐   iii) £66 = ☐ AED

ii) 55 AED = £ ☐   iv) £990 = ☐ AED

b) Some perfume in Dubai costs 220 AED. The same perfume in the UK costs £55

Where is the perfume cheaper to buy?

_____

5   The graph shows the conversion of temperature between Celsius and Fahrenheit.

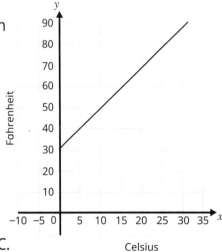

a) On 1st January, the temperature in Greenland is 25°F.

Use the graph to make an approximate conversion of this temperature to degrees Celsius.

☐

b) On 1st July, the mean daily temperature in the UK is 20°C.

In July, the mean daily temperature in Greece is 85°F.

Use the graph to work out an approximate difference in temperature between the UK and Greece in July.

☐

11

6   Ron goes on holiday to Spain.

The exchange rate between pounds and euros is £1 = €1.15

Ron buys £150 worth of euros.

He spends €200 and converts the rest back to pounds at the same rate.

How much money does he get back?   £ [   ]

7   **H**   a) i)   On Graph A, draw an example of a direct proportion relationship.

   ii)   On Graph B, draw an example of a relationship that is not in direct proportion.

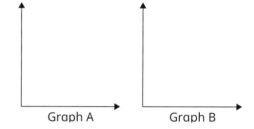

Graph A   Graph B

b)   Explain why your line on Graph B does not show direct proportion.

_____

8   **H**   Tick the tables that show direct proportion.

a)

Distance (miles)	13	26	7
Cost (£)	18.2	36.4	9.8

b)

Height (cm)	15	35	89
Width (cm)	27	56	146.85

c)

Distance (miles)	22	50	78
Cost (£)	52.8	120	187.2

9   **H**   Complete the table to show a direct proportional relationship.

x		8	20	
y	10.2	27.2		425

How did you find these questions?

Very easy   1   2   3   4   5   6   7   8   9   10   Very difficult

Multiplicative change

Date:

Let's remember

1   12 cupcakes cost £15. How much do 5 cupcakes cost?

£ _____

2   Write the ratio 30 : 18 in its simplest form.   ☐ : ☐

3   Find the highest common factor (HCF) of 32 and 56   ☐

4   Work out the size of angle x ☐ °

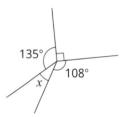

135°   108° x

Let's practise

1   Work out the missing lengths in these pairs of similar shapes.

a)

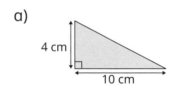

4 cm
10 cm

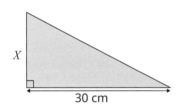

X
30 cm

$X =$ _____ cm

b)

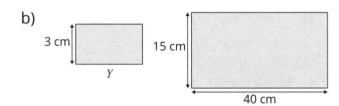

3 cm
Y

15 cm
40 cm

$Y =$ _____ cm

c)

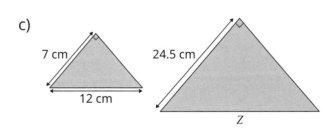

7 cm
12 cm

24.5 cm
Z

$Z =$ _____ cm

2 These two shapes are similar.

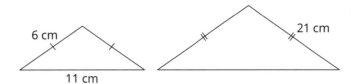

a) Work out the perimeter of the smaller triangle.

perimeter = ☐ cm

b) Work out the perimeter of the larger triangle.

perimeter = ☐ cm

c) Write the ratio of the perimeter of the smaller triangle to the larger triangle in the form $1:n$

☐ : ☐

3 For each pair of similar shapes, write the scale factor of the lengths from shape A to shape B.

a)

Scale factor = ☐

2 cm   10 cm

b)

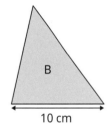

Scale factor = ☐

c)

Scale factor = ☐

4   A triangle has a base of 8 cm and a perpendicular height of 5 cm.

Work out the base length and height for enlargements with the given scale factors.

a) Scale factor = 4

base = [   ] cm   height = [   ] cm

b) Scale factor = 0.5

base = [   ] cm   height = [   ] cm

c) Scale factor = $\frac{3}{4}$

base = [   ] cm   height = [   ] cm

5   The scale on a diagram is such that 5 cm represents 1 m.

a) What does 15 cm on the diagram represent? [   ] m

b) What does 25 cm on the diagram represent? [   ] m

c) What does 1 cm on the diagram represent? [   ] m

d) What does 3.2 cm on the diagram represent? [   ] m

How did you find these questions?

Very easy   1   2   3   4   5   6   7   8   9   10   Very difficult

Block 3 Multiplying and dividing fractions

In this block, you will build on work you have already done on multiplying and dividing **fractions**. You will use **bar models** to help you to multiply and divide integers by fractions. For example, this one shows $3 \div \frac{1}{4}$

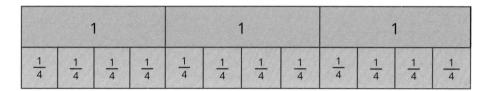

You work out how to multiply a fraction by an **integer**.

This bar model and number line shows how you can find $\frac{2}{3} \times 4$

You can see that the answer is $2\frac{2}{3}$

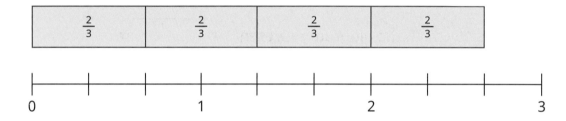

You also divide fractions. For example, $\frac{2}{3} \div \frac{1}{18} = 12$

Can you see how this bar model shows that?

$\frac{1}{3}$						$\frac{1}{3}$						$\frac{1}{3}$					
$\frac{1}{18}$	$\frac{1}{18}$	$\frac{1}{18}$	$\frac{1}{18}$	$\frac{1}{18}$	$\frac{1}{18}$	$\frac{1}{18}$	$\frac{1}{18}$	$\frac{1}{18}$	$\frac{1}{18}$	$\frac{1}{18}$	$\frac{1}{18}$	$\frac{1}{18}$	$\frac{1}{18}$	$\frac{1}{18}$	$\frac{1}{18}$	$\frac{1}{18}$	$\frac{1}{18}$

You work out how to calculate with fractions without using a bar model or number line. This calculation is an example

$$2\frac{1}{4} \div \frac{3}{5} = 3\frac{3}{4}$$

Key vocabulary

Fraction   Numerator   Denominator   Integer   Mixed number

Proper fraction   Improper fraction   Unit fraction   Reciprocal

Multiplying and dividing fractions

Date:

Let's remember

1. Work out the missing length x in the similar shapes.

   [ ] cm

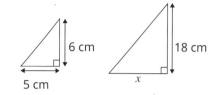

2. The currency in Australia is the Australian dollar ($).

   £1 = $1.76

   Convert £15 to Australian dollars.

   $ [ ]

3. Purple paint is made by mixing blue and red paint in the ratio 2:3

   If 600 ml of red paint is used, how much blue paint is needed?

   [ ] ml

4. Three interior angles of a quadrilateral are 78°, 143° and 96°.

   Work out the size of the fourth interior angle.

   [ ] °

Let's practise

1. a) What addition does the blue (B) represent in the diagram?

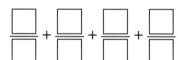

   b) What multiplication does the blue (B) represent in the diagram?

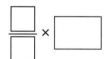

B	B	B		
B	B	B		
B	B	B		
B	B	B		

2 Use the diagram to work out $\frac{2}{5} \times 3$

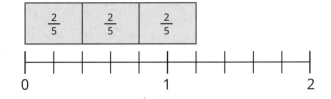

Give your answer as an improper fraction
and as a mixed number.

$$\frac{\boxed{}}{\boxed{}} = \boxed{}\frac{\boxed{}}{\boxed{}}$$

3 Complete the calculations.

Give your answers as mixed numbers in their simplest form where appropriate.

a) $5 \times \frac{1}{3} = \dfrac{\boxed{}}{\boxed{}} = \boxed{}\dfrac{\boxed{}}{\boxed{}}$

c) $\frac{2}{5} \times 7 = \dfrac{\boxed{}}{\boxed{}} = \boxed{}\dfrac{\boxed{}}{\boxed{}}$

b) $6 \times \frac{3}{4} = \dfrac{\boxed{}}{\boxed{}} = \boxed{}\dfrac{\boxed{}}{\boxed{}}$

d) $12 \times \frac{5}{8} = \dfrac{\boxed{}}{\boxed{}} = \boxed{}\dfrac{\boxed{}}{\boxed{}}$

4 A tin of cat food weighs $\frac{2}{5}$ kg.

Mr Dean buys eight tins of cat food.

What is the total mass of all eight tins?

Give your answer as a mixed number.

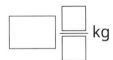 kg

5 Find the missing numbers in the calculations.

a) $\frac{3}{11} \times \boxed{} = \frac{6}{11}$

c) $\dfrac{\boxed{}}{\boxed{}} \times 6 = \frac{18}{5} = \boxed{}\dfrac{\boxed{}}{\boxed{}}$

b) $\boxed{} \times \frac{4}{7} = \frac{12}{7} = 1\frac{5}{7}$

d) $\boxed{} \times \frac{5}{6} = \dfrac{\boxed{}}{\boxed{}} = 5\frac{5}{6}$

6 Complete the calculations.

a) $\frac{1}{5} \times \frac{1}{2} = \dfrac{\boxed{}}{\boxed{}}$

d) $\frac{1}{4} \times \frac{1}{\boxed{}} = \frac{1}{20}$

b) $\frac{1}{3} \times \frac{1}{7} = \dfrac{\boxed{}}{\boxed{}}$

e) $\frac{1}{\boxed{}} \times 0.1 = \frac{1}{70}$

c) $(\frac{1}{8})^2 = \dfrac{\boxed{}}{\boxed{}}$

f) $0.5 \times \dfrac{\boxed{}}{2} = \frac{1}{4}$

7 A piece of wood is $\frac{1}{2}$ metre long. Dani uses $\frac{1}{3}$ of the piece of wood.

a) What fraction of a metre does Dani use?

 m

b) What fraction of a metre is left?

Give your answer in its simplest form.

 m

8 Complete the calculations. Simplify your answers where possible.

a) $\frac{4}{5} \times \frac{2}{3} = \dfrac{\boxed{}}{\boxed{}}$

d) $\frac{3}{7} \times \dfrac{8}{\boxed{}} = \frac{24}{77}$

b) $\frac{3}{4} \times \frac{5}{6} = \dfrac{\boxed{}}{\boxed{}}$

e) $\dfrac{\boxed{}}{12} \times \frac{5}{8} = \frac{35}{96}$

c) $\left(\frac{3}{5}\right)^2 = \dfrac{\boxed{}}{\boxed{}}$

f) $\frac{9}{20} \times \frac{5}{18} = \dfrac{\boxed{}}{\boxed{}}$

9 Complete the calculations. You can use a bar model like this to help you.

1	1	1

$\frac{1}{4}$	$\frac{1}{4}$	$\frac{1}{4}$	$\frac{1}{4}$	$\frac{1}{4}$	$\frac{1}{4}$	$\frac{1}{4}$	$\frac{1}{4}$	$\frac{1}{4}$	$\frac{1}{4}$	$\frac{1}{4}$	$\frac{1}{4}$

a) $1 \div \frac{1}{4} = \boxed{}$ b) $2 \div \frac{1}{4} = \boxed{}$ c) $3 \div \frac{1}{4} = \boxed{}$ d) $3 \div \frac{3}{4} = \boxed{}$

10 Complete the calculations.

a) $4 \div \frac{2}{3} = \boxed{}$ b) $8 \div \frac{4}{5} = \boxed{}$ c) $6 \div \frac{3}{8} = \boxed{}$ d) $12 \div \frac{3}{7} = \boxed{}$

11 Work out the values if $a = \frac{1}{4}$ and $b = \frac{2}{3}$

a) $5a = \dfrac{\boxed{}}{\boxed{}} = \boxed{}\dfrac{\boxed{}}{\boxed{}}$

c) $5b = \dfrac{\boxed{}}{\boxed{}} = \boxed{}\dfrac{\boxed{}}{\boxed{}}$

b) $\frac{5}{a} = \boxed{}$

d) $\frac{5}{b} = \dfrac{\boxed{}}{\boxed{}} = \boxed{}\dfrac{\boxed{}}{\boxed{}}$

How did you find these questions?

Very easy   1   2   3   4   5   6   7   8   9   10   Very difficult

Multiplying and dividing fractions

Date:

Let's remember

1   Work out $\frac{2}{5} \times \frac{3}{7}$ $\frac{\boxed{}}{\boxed{}}$

2   A rectangle has a length of 7 cm and a width of 4 cm.

Work out the length and width of the rectangle if it is enlarged by a scale factor of 3

length = $\boxed{}$ cm   width = $\boxed{}$ cm

3   Write the ratio 12:3 in the form $n:1$

$\boxed{} : \boxed{}$

4   Two angles in a triangle are 72° and 53°

What is the size of the third angle? $\boxed{}$°

Let's practise

1   Use the fraction wall to complete the calculations.

$\frac{1}{2}$				$\frac{1}{2}$			
$\frac{1}{4}$		$\frac{1}{4}$		$\frac{1}{4}$		$\frac{1}{4}$	
$\frac{1}{8}$	$\frac{1}{8}$	$\frac{1}{8}$	$\frac{1}{8}$	$\frac{1}{8}$	$\frac{1}{8}$	$\frac{1}{8}$	$\frac{1}{8}$

a) $\frac{1}{2} \div \frac{1}{4} = \boxed{}$

c) $\frac{3}{4} \div \frac{1}{8} = \boxed{}$

b) $\frac{1}{2} \div \frac{1}{8} = \boxed{}$

d) $\frac{5}{4} \div \frac{1}{8} = \boxed{}$

2   Complete the calculations.

a) $\frac{2}{3} \div \frac{1}{18} = \boxed{}$

b) $\frac{5}{6} \div \frac{1}{18} = \boxed{}$

c) $\frac{7}{9} \div \frac{1}{18} = \boxed{}$

3   Write the reciprocal of each of the numbers.

a) 5 $\boxed{}$

c) $\frac{1}{4}$ $\boxed{}$

b) y $\boxed{}$

d) $\frac{4}{5}$ $\boxed{}$

4 Complete the calculations.

Write your answers as mixed numbers in their simplest form, where appropriate.

a) $\frac{5}{8} \div \frac{3}{4} = \boxed{}$

d) $\frac{2}{3} \div \frac{7}{12} = \boxed{}$

b) $\frac{3}{4} \div \frac{5}{8} = \boxed{}$

e) $\frac{5}{6} \div 4 = \boxed{}$

c) $\frac{7}{12} \div \frac{2}{3} = \boxed{}$

f) $6 \div \frac{4}{5} = \boxed{}$

5 a) Write each decimal as a fraction.

i) $0.3 = \dfrac{\boxed{}}{\boxed{}}$

ii) $0.7 = \dfrac{\boxed{}}{\boxed{}}$

b) Complete the calculations.

Give your answers as mixed numbers in their simplest form.

i) $5 \div 0.7 = \boxed{}$

ii) $8 \div 0.3 = \boxed{}$

6 Complete the calculations.

H

Write your answers as mixed numbers in their simplest form where appropriate.

a) $1\frac{1}{2} \times \frac{1}{3} = \boxed{}$

e) $3\frac{5}{6} \times 4 = \boxed{}$

b) $2\frac{3}{4} \times \frac{1}{5} = \boxed{}$

f) $2\frac{2}{3} \times 1\frac{3}{4} = \boxed{}$

c) $\frac{2}{3} \times 5\frac{2}{3} = \boxed{}$

g) $3\frac{3}{4} \times 5\frac{1}{2} = \boxed{}$

d) $3 \times 4\frac{1}{5} = \boxed{}$

h) $(3\frac{1}{2})^2 = \boxed{}$

7 Complete the calculations.

H

Write your answers as mixed numbers in their simplest form where appropriate.

a) $5\frac{1}{2} \div 3 = \boxed{}$

c) $9\frac{1}{2} \div 3\frac{1}{6} = \boxed{}$

b) $5\frac{1}{3} \div 4\frac{1}{3} = \boxed{}$

d) $7\frac{1}{5} \div 3\frac{1}{10} = \boxed{}$

8 Work out the values, if $a = \frac{1}{5}$, $b = \frac{2}{3}$ and $c = 1\frac{3}{4}$

Write your answers as proper fractions or as mixed numbers in their simplest form where appropriate.

a) $ab = \boxed{}$

d) $\frac{c}{a} = \boxed{}$

b) $\frac{a}{b} = \boxed{}$

e) $abc = \boxed{}$

c) $ac = \boxed{}$

f) $\frac{bc}{a} = \boxed{}$

9 Simplify the calculations.

a) $h \times \frac{1}{4} = \frac{\boxed{}}{\boxed{}}$

d) $\frac{w}{4} \times \frac{y}{7} = \frac{\boxed{}}{\boxed{}}$

b) $\frac{2}{3} \times g = \frac{\boxed{}}{\boxed{}}$

e) $\frac{7}{10} \times 3 \times \frac{p}{4} = \frac{\boxed{}}{\boxed{}}$

c) $\frac{m}{5} \times \frac{3}{n} = \frac{\boxed{}}{\boxed{}}$

10 Complete the calculations. Give the answers in their simplest form.

a) $\frac{x}{7} \div 3 = \boxed{}$

d) $\frac{x}{3} \div 7x = \boxed{}$

b) $\frac{7}{x} \div 3 = \boxed{}$

e) $\frac{x}{3} \div \frac{x}{7} = \boxed{}$

c) $\frac{7}{x} \div x = \boxed{}$

f) $\frac{x}{3} \div \frac{7}{x} = \boxed{}$

How did you find these questions?

Very easy   1   2   3   4   5   6   7   8   9   10   Very difficult

Block 4 Working in the Cartesian plane

In this block, you build on your knowledge of **coordinates**, and you will start to draw **straight line graphs**. You use x and y **axes** drawn on a square grid, like this.

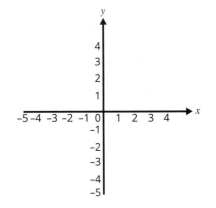

You practise drawing **vertical** and **horizontal** lines. One of these lines is **parallel** to the x axis. Can you see which one it is?

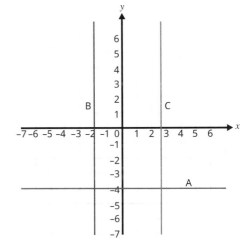

You also explore **diagonal** graph lines, like these. They all have the same **gradient**, meaning that they are parallel. A line can have a positive or negative gradient, this tells you which direction the slope is.

You use a **table of values** to work out the coordinates from an equation. Once you know the coordinates, you can plot a graph. Here's a table of values for the equation $y = 3 - x$

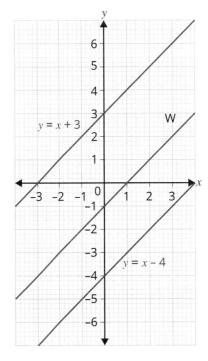

x	−2	−1	0	1	2
y	5	4	3	2	1

You will also find the midpoint of two points. To do this, you can find the coordinates that lie exactly half way between the x-coordinates and the y-coordinates of the points.

Key vocabulary

Coordinates   Straight line graph   Axis/Axes   Vertical   Horizontal   Gradient

Diagonal   Table of values   Quadrant   Equation   Midpoint   Parallel

Working in the Cartesian plane

Date:

Let's remember

1 Work out $\frac{3}{4} \div \frac{1}{8}$ ☐

2 Work out $\frac{3}{5} \times 7$

   Give your answer as a mixed number. ☐ ☐/☐

3 7 pints is approximately equal to 4 litres.

   Approximately how many litres is 35 pints? ☐ l

4 180 + 430 = ☐

Let's practise

1 a) Write the coordinates of points G, H and J.

   G = _____

   H = _____

   J = _____

   b) Plot the points on the grid.

      A (–3, 1)

      B (–4, –3)

      C (–2, –3)

   c) Join points A, B and C to form a triangle.

      What type of triangle is ABC?

      _____

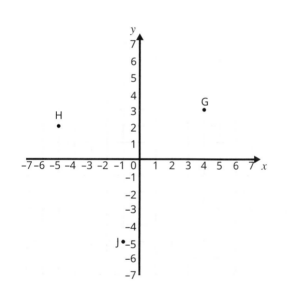

24

2   a) Tick the coordinates that do **not** lie in the fourth quadrant.

   (3, –4)   (4, –3)   (–3, 4)   (5, –3)

   b) Tick the coordinates that lie on the line $y = -3$

   (3, –4)   (4, –3)   (–3, 4)   (5, –3)

3   Tick the lines that pass through the point (5, –8)

   $x = 5$ $y = 5$ $x = -8$ $y = -8$

4   Here is a blank coordinate grid.

   a) Draw the line $x = 1$ on the grid.

   b) Draw the line $y = -2$ on the same grid.

   c) Write the coordinates of the point where the

      lines $x = 1$ and $y = -2$ intersect.

      _____

   d) Draw the line $y = x$ on the same grid.

   e) Write the coordinates of a point on the line $y = x$ that you cannot see on the grid.

      _____

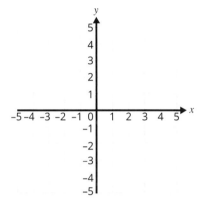

5   a) Which two lines are parallel to each other?

   b) Which line is parallel to the x-axis?

   c) Write the equation of each line.

      A:

      B: _____

      C: _____

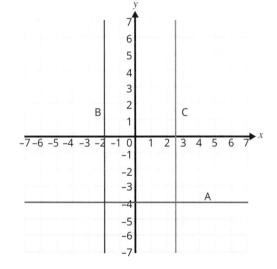

6   a) Tick the points that lie on the line $y = x$

      (3, 6)   (6, 6)   (3, 12)   (6, 30)

   b) Tick the points that lie on the line $y = 4x$

      (3, 6)   (6, 6)   (3, 12)   (6, 30)

7   a) Complete the table of values for $y = 5x$

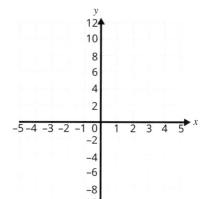

x	−2	−1	0	1	2
y					

b) Plot the graph of $y = 5x$

c) Complete the sentence.

> On the graph $y = 5x$, the y-coordinate is always ☐ times the x-coordinate.

8   Tick the graph that is the steepest.

$y = \frac{1}{7}x$ $y = 7x$ $y = 7$ $y = 17x$

9   Tick the graphs that could show $y = x$

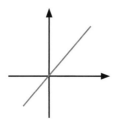   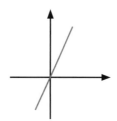   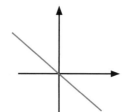   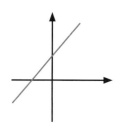

10   Two congruent rectangles are shown.

Work out the coordinates of X and Y.

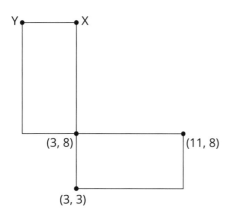

X = _____   Y = _____

How did you find these questions?

Very easy   1   2   3   4   5   6   7   8   9   10   Very difficult

26

Working in the Cartesian plane

Date:

Let's remember

1. Circle the point that lies on the line $y = 5$

   (5, −1)   (−5, 5)   (1, −5)   (5, −5)

2. Work out $\frac{2}{3} \div \frac{1}{6}$ ☐

3. A scale drawing is such that 1 cm represents 5 m.

   What does 12 cm represent? ☐ m

4. Use the fact that: 74 × 13 = 962 to work out 740 × 130

   ☐

Let's practise

1. Cupcakes are sold in boxes.

   Each box contains 6 cupcakes.

   a) i) How many cupcakes are in 8 boxes?

   ☐

   ii) How many cupcakes are in 0 boxes?

   ☐

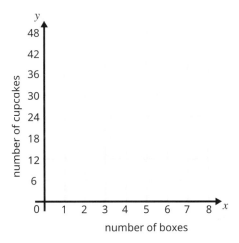

   b) Plot a graph to show the number of cupcakes as the number of boxes increases.

   c) What is the equation of the line that you have drawn?

   _____

2. Tick the equations that have graphs that are steeper than the graph of $y = 3x$

   $y = 2x$ $y = 4x$ $y = \frac{1}{3}x$ $y = 30x$

27

3 a) Write the equation of line W. _____

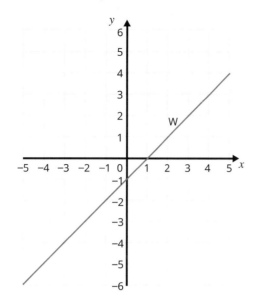

b) Complete each table of values.

i) $y = x + 3$

x	-2	-1	0	1	2
y					

ii) $y = x - 4$

x	-2	-1	0	1	2
y					

c) Plot both lines on the axes. Label your lines.

d) What do you notice about the three lines?

_____

4 Tick the coordinates that lie on the line $y = x + 5$

(0, –5)   (0, 5)   (–5, 0)   (5, 0)   (8, 3)   (3, 8)

5 Tick the graph that could show the line $y = -x$

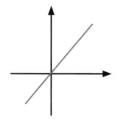   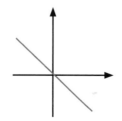   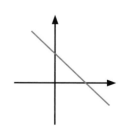

6   a) Complete each table of values.

i) $y = 3 - x$

x	-2	-1	0	1	2
y					

ii) $y = -3 - x$

x	-2	-1	0	1	2
y					

iii) $y = -3x$

x	-2	-1	0	1	2
y					

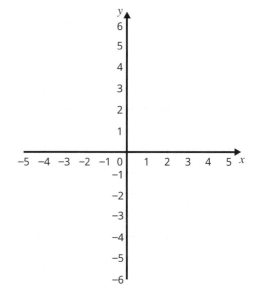

b) Plot all three lines on the axes.

7   Find the equation of the line that passes through the point (2, 4) and the origin.

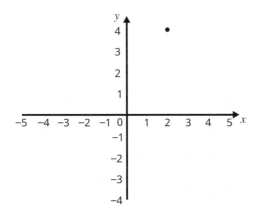

_____

8   Tick the equations that have a negative gradient.

| $y = -2x - 5$ | $-5 + 2x = y$ | $y - 2x = 5$ |

| $y + 2x = -5$ | $5 - 2x = y$ |

How did you find these questions?

Very easy   1   2   3   4   5   6   7   8   9   10   Very difficult

Working in the Cartesian plane

Date:

Let's remember

1   Circle all the coordinates that lie on the line $y = x - 5$

(0, 5)   (4, 9)   (9, 4)   (0, −5)   (−5, 0)

2   Write the coordinates of a point that lies on the line $y = x$ _____

3   Work out $\frac{1}{5} \div \frac{1}{3}$ $\dfrac{\square}{\square}$

4   Write the ratio $18:12$ in its simplest form. _____

Let's practise

1   Here is a sequence.

7, 9, 11, 13, 15, ...

The 1st term is 7, so this term of the sequence can be written using the coordinates (1, 7).

a) Write the coordinates for each term of the sequence.

2nd term = _____   4th term = _____

3rd term = _____   5th term = _____

b) Complete the table of values for $y = 2x + 5$

x	1	2	3	4	5
y					

c) What do you notice about the sequence and the line $y = 2x + 5$?

_____

2 A sequence is made using squares. Here are
   thre first three terms of the sequence.

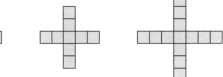

a) Write three coordinates to describe the sequence.

_____

b) Plot your points on the grid and join them up using a ruler.

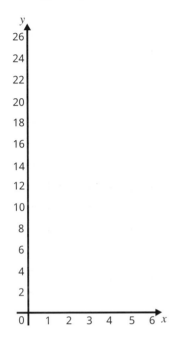

c) Use your graph to write the coordinates for the 6th term of the sequence.

_____

3 a) Complete each table of values.

i) $y = 2x - 3$

x	-2	-1	0	1	2
y					

ii) $y = -3x + 2$

x	-2	-1	0	1	2
y					

iii) $y = \frac{1}{2}x - 2$

x	-2	-1	0	1	2
y					

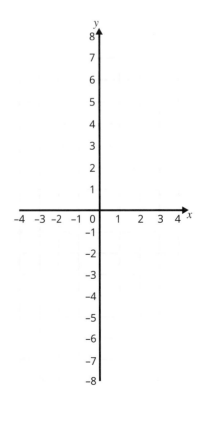

b) Plot the lines on the axes. Label your lines.

31

4 Match each coordinate with the equation of the line it could lie on.

$y = 5 - 4x$		(5, –3)
$y = \dfrac{x}{5} - 4$		(6, 2)
$y = \dfrac{x + 4}{5}$		(2, –3)

5 Tick the equations that form non-linear graphs.

$y = 2x^2$ $y = x + 2$ $y = \dfrac{x}{2}$ $y = x^2$

$y = 2x$ $y = x^3$ $y = -x^2$ $2 - x = y$

6 a) Find the midpoints of these pairs of points.

   i)   (0, 0) and (6, 8) _____   iii) (8, –3) and (–2, 13) _____

   ii) (3, 4) and (–1, 6) _____   iv) (–7, 5) and (–3, –2) _____

   b) Find the midpoint of the points (m, n) and $(5m, -2n)$ _____

7 A line segment starts at (1, 4). It has a midpoint of (–1, 6)

   What are the coordinates of the end point of the line? _____

8 A line passes through the points G (0, 8) and H (4, 0)

   a) Find the equation of the line. _____

   b) Another line passes through point G and J (–8, 0)

      Find the equation of the line segment GJ. _____

How did you find these questions?

Very easy   1   2   3   4   5   6   7   8   9   10   Very difficult

Block 5 Representing data

In this block, you learn about different ways of representing **data**. You start with **scatter graphs**, which are a great way of showing if there's any **correlation** between two sets of data. That means if you can see a pattern, like in this graph.

You explore **lines of best fit**. This scatter graph shows the weight and length of boxes in a warehouse. The line of best fit allows us to **predict**, for example, the length of a box that has a weight of 70 kg.

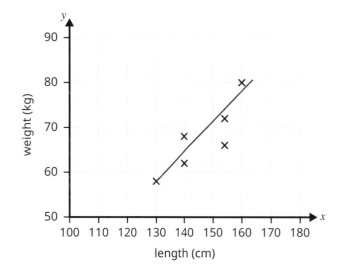

You also work with **frequency tables**. This table shows the pets kept by a class of students. Can you work out how many pets there are altogether?

Type of pet	Frequency
Dog	9
Cat	7
Fish	5
Rabbit	3

You explore **two-way tables**. This one shows the number of animals on a farm, but there are some numbers missing. Can you work out how many sheep there are in total?

	Male	Female	Total
Horses	67		154
Chickens	76	61	
Sheep	49		
Total		220	

Key vocabulary

Data   Scatter graph   Correlation   Line of best fit

Predict   Frequency table   Two-way table   Discrete   Continuous

Representing data

Date:

Let's remember

1. Tick the linear sequences.

   2, 4, 8, 16, …   2, 4, 6, 8, …   2, 0, −2, −4, …   0.2, 0.4, 0.6, 0.8, …

2. Max gets paid £60 for 5 hours work.

   How much does he get paid per hour?   £ ☐

3. Write the reciprocal of 6 ☐

4. There are 6 red counters and 5 blue counters in a bag.

   A counter is selected at random.

   Work out the probability of selecting a red counter. _____

Let's practise

1. Draw lines to match the graphs to the correct description.

   | Strong positive correlation |

   | Weak positive correlation |

   | Strong negative correlation |

   | Weak negative correlation |

   | No correlation |

2 a) Tick the correct line of best fit for the graph.

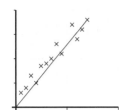
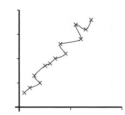

   b) Tick the correct line of best fit for the graph.

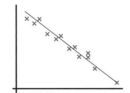
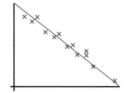

3   The scatter graph shows information about the weight and the length of some boxes in a warehouse.

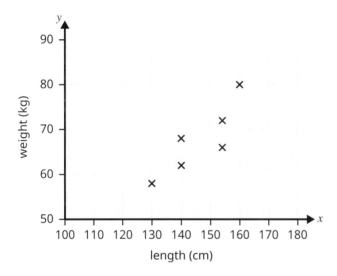

   a) How many boxes are shown on the graph?

   The table shows the weight and length of three more boxes.

Length (cm)	146	150	172
Weight (kg)	66	78	84

   b) On the scatter graph, plot the information from the table.

   c) i) What type of correlation does this scatter graph show? _____

      ii) What does this tell you about the relationship betwen the weight and length of these boxes?

   _____

d) Use a ruler to draw the line of best fit.

e) Use your line of best fit to predict the length of a box with a weight of 70 kg.

predicted length = [　　　　] cm

f) Explain why your prediction in part e) is only an estimate.

_____

4   The scatter graph shows information about some cars.

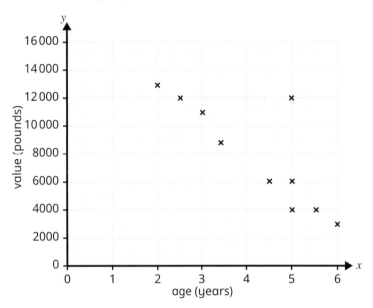

a) Circle the outlier on the graph.

b) Another car is 4 years old and is worth £8000

   Show this information on the scatter graph.

c) Describe the correlation between the values of the cars and the ages of the cars.

_____

_____

d) Use a ruler to draw the line of best fit.

e) Use your line of best fit to predict the value of a car that is 3.5 years old.

£ [　　　　　　]

How did you find these questions?

Very easy   1   2   3   4   5   6   7   8   9   10   Very difficult

Representing data

Date:

Let's remember

1   Tick the graph that shows negative correlation.

A   B   C

2   Complete the table of values for $y = 2x - 1$

x	0	1	2	3
y				

3   Write the coordinates of two points that lie on the line $y = x$

_____

4   Circle the prime numbers.

1   2   3   4   5   6   7   8   9

Let's practise

1   The table shows the pets kept by a class of students.

Type of pet	Frequency
Dog	9
Cat	7
Fish	5
Rabbit	3

a) Which animal is the most popular pet? _____

b) How many different types of animals do the class keep as pets?

c) How many pets are there altogether?

37

2   Some students were asked how long they take to walk to school, to the nearest minute.

The table shows some information about the results.

Time (minutes)	Frequency
0 to 10	9
11 to 20	15
21 to 30	5
31 to 40	3

a) How many students take 11 to 20 minutes to walk to school?

b) How many students were asked?

c) How many students take less than 31 minutes to walk to school?

d) Why can't you tell exactly how many students take less than 5 minutes to walk to school?

_____

_____

3   The masses of 20 pumpkins are recorded.

4.1 kg   6.7 kg   5.8 kg   12.2 kg   7.3 kg   15.1 kg   18.2 kg   6.7 kg   8.9 kg   11.1 kg

17.6 kg   8.9 kg   4.8 kg   9.2 kg   5.3 kg   17.6 kg   16.1 kg   9.9 kg   5.6 kg   8.7 kg

a) Complete the table.

Mass (kg)	Tally	Frequency
$0 < t \leq 5$		
$5 < t \leq 10$		
$10 < t \leq 15$		
$15 < t \leq 20$		

b) Use the table to work out how many pumpkins have a mass that is more than 5 kg.

c) Which interval has the highest frequency? _____

d) What percentage of pumpkins have a mass that is less than or equal to 15 kg?

4   The two-way table shows the number of animals on a farm.

	Male	Female	Total
Horses	67		154
Chickens	76	61	
Sheep	49		
Total		220	

a) Complete the two-way table.

b) How many of the animals are males?

c) How many chickens are there on the farm?

d) How many animals are there in total?

5   Olivia asks 100 students what their favourite lesson is out of history, geography or languages.

47 of the students are in Year 7

34 of these Year 7 students say history is their favourite subject.

21 Year 8 students say history is their favourite subject.

3 out of the 17 students whose favourite subject is languages are in Year 7

a) Draw and complete a two-way table to show this information.

b) How many students said that geography is their favourite subject?

c) What fraction of the students picked history as their favourite subject?
    Give your answer in its simplest form.

How did you find these questions?

Very easy   1   2   3   4   5   6   7   8   9   10   Very difficult

Block 6   Tables & probability

In this block, you build on the work you did last year on **probability**. You start by listing **outcomes**, which you can do with a **sample space diagram**. Here's one that is partly filled in for these two bags of counters, where one counter is chosen at **random** from each bag.

		Bag 2		
		Red	Blue	Green
Bag 1	1	(1, R)		
	2	(2, R)		
	3			

You can see how the **two-way tables** that you have recently learned about can help you to work out probabilities. This one gives information about the cakes in a shop.

	Chocolate	Lemon	Total
Small	28		54
Medium		39	
Large	47	31	
Total			200

You use **Venn diagrams** to solve real-life problems. This one shows 32 students who were asked whether they have a sister or a brother. The **intersection** of the Venn diagram shows that 7 students have a sister and a brother. You can see that the probability that a randomly chosen student doesn't have a sister is $\frac{3}{8}$

Can you see how to work that out?

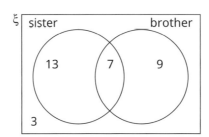

Key vocabulary

Probability   Outcomes   Sample space   diagram   Random   Formula/Formulae

Two-way table   Venn diagram   Intersection   Set

Tables & probability

Date:

Let's remember

1   The two-way table shows how some students travel to school. Complete the table.

	Walk	Bus	Other	Total
Students in Year 7	36		32	126
Students in Year 8		31	17	
Total	74			212

2   Draw the line of best fit on the scatter graph.

3   Tick the equations that have a negative gradient.

$y = 3x$ $y = -3x$ $y = -x$ $y = x - 3$ $y = 3 - x$

4   Mo says that the total of the scores on two dice is always even.
Give an example of when Mo's statement is incorrect.

_____

Let's practise

1   Alex has two bags of counters. She chooses one counter at random from each bag.

a) Complete the sample space diagram for the possible outcomes.

		Bag 2		
		Red	Blue	Green
	1	(1, R)		
Bag 1	2			
	3			

b) How many possible outcomes are there? ☐

c) How many of the outcomes contain a number 2? ☐

d) Fill in the missing information.

i) P(2, B) = _____

ii) P(3) = _____

41

2   Amir rolls two dice and multiplies the numbers to give a score.

a) Complete the sample space diagram.

		Dice 2					
		1	**2**	**3**	**4**	**5**	**6**
Dice 1	**1**						
	2						
	3						
	4						
	5						
	6						

b) Are there more even or more odd outcomes? _____

c) Complete the probabilities.

   i) P(score of 6) = _____

   ii) P(score of more than 10) = _____

   iii) P(odd number) = _____

3   A shop makes three sizes of cakes. The sizes are small, medium and large.

Each cake can be chocolate flavour or lemon flavour.

The two-way table shows the number of cakes the shop makes in 1 week.

	Chocolate	Lemon	Total
Small	28		54
Medium		39	
Large	47	31	
Total			200

a) Complete the missing values in the two-way table.

b) A cake is selected at random.

   i) Work out the probability that it is a small lemon cake.

   _____

   ii) What is the probability that the cake is medium in size?

   _____

4   Shade the Venn diagrams to show the correct statement.

a) A ∪ B

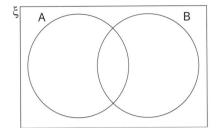

b) A

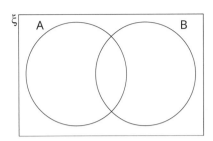

5   a) Sort the numbers 1, 2, 3, 4, 5, 6, 7, 8, 9 and 10 into the Venn diagram.

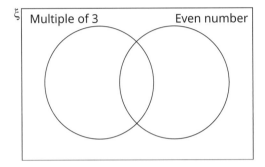

b) A number is chosen at random.

Find the probability it is

i)   a multiple of 3 = _____

ii) a multiple of 3 and even = _____

6   32 students were asked whether they have a sister or brother.

The Venn diagram shows the results.

A student is chosen at random.

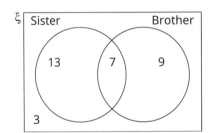

a) Fill in the missing information.

i) P(sister) = _____

ii) P(sister and brother) = _____

iii) P(does not have a brother) = _____

iv) P(has a sister but not a brother) = _____

b) A student has a sister.

What is the probability that they do not have a brother? _____

How did you find these questions?

Very easy   1   2   3   4   5   6   7   8   9   10   Very difficult

Autumn term   Self-assessment

Time to reflect

Look back through the work you have done this term. Think about what you enjoyed and what you found easy or hard. Talk about this to your teacher and someone at home.

Try these questions	How do you feel about this topic? Tick the box.
The two triangles are similar. Find the value of x $x =$ ☐ If you need a reminder, look back at multiplicative change on pages 9–15 4 cm, 3 cm, 14 cm, x	☐ I am confident and could teach someone else. ☐ I think I understand but I need practice. ☐ I don't understand and need help.

a) Complete the table of values for the equation $y = 4x$

x	–2	–1	0	1	2
y					

b) Hence, plot the graph of $y = 4x$ on the axes.

If you need a reminder, look back at the working in the Cartesian plane on pages 23–32

☐ I am confident and could teach someone else.

☐ I think I understand but I need practice.

☐ I don't understand and need help.

The scatter graph shows the length and mass of some pebbles on a beach. By drawing a line of best fit, estimate the mass of a pebble that is 20 mm in length.

mass ≈ ☐ g

If you need a reminder, look back at pages 33–43

mass of pebble (g) vs *length of pebble (mm)*

☐ I am confident and could teach someone else.

☐ I think I understand but I need practice.

☐ I don't understand and need help.

Block 1 Brackets, equations & inequalities

In this block, you build on the work you did on **algebra** last year. You can use shapes to represent **terms**, which you can then add or subtract to make **expressions,** like here.

$\square$ = $2h$

$\bigcirc$ = $5g$

$\square$ $\square$ $\square$ $\bigcirc$ $\bigcirc$ $\bigcirc$ $\bigcirc$ = $\boxed{6h + 20g}$

You use bar models to **expand brackets**. This one shows $3(y + 5)$

y	5
y	5
y	5

You also use bar models to help you **factorise** expressions.

This one helps you to factorise $18t + 24$

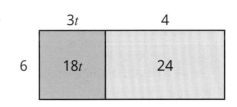

You build on your knowledge of how to **solve equations**, including in problems like this one. Here, the area of the rectangle is 70 cm² and you have to work out y

5 cm | 70 cm²

$2(4y - 3)$

You will use **inequalities**. $t \leq 9$ means that the value of t is less than or equal to 9.
You can also solve inequalities. This example shows how to solve $4b + 1 < 7$

$4b + 1 < 7$

$4b < 8$

$b < 2$

Key vocabulary

Algebra   Expression   Term   Expand   Brackets   Factorise   Formula/Formulae

Solve   Equation   Inequality   Simplify   Like terms

Brackets, equations & inequalities

Date:

Let's remember

1 An ice cream shop has 3 flavours of ice cream and 2 toppings.

H How many different combinations are there? ☐

2 The masses of 20 animals are recorded.

Mass (kg)	$0 < t \leq 5$	$5 < t \leq 10$	$10 < t \leq 15$	$15 < t \leq 20$
Frequency	1	14	3	2

How many animals have a mass that is greater than 10 kg? ☐

3 Write the coordinates of a point that lies on the line $y = 5x$ _____

4 A bag contains red and blue counters.

The ratio of red to blue counters is $1:3$

There are 12 red counters.

How many blue counters are there? ☐

Let's practise

1 Match each algebraic expression with the correct description.

$3y$	y less than 3
$y + 3$	3 less than y
$3 - y$	3 more than y
$y - 3$	y multiplied by 3

2 Whitney has p pounds. She spends r pounds.

a) Write an expression for how much money she has now.

_____

b) Whitney buys a book for m pounds and three pens for n pounds each.

Write an expression for the total cost of the book and three pens.

_____

3   $= 2h$

⬤ $= 5g$

Write an expression for the total, giving your answers as simply as possible.

a)

_____

b) ▪ ▪ ▪

⬤ ⬤ ⬤ ⬤

_____

4 Work out the value of the expressions when $x = 4$ and $y = -8$

a) $x + y = \boxed{}$

b) $xy = \boxed{}$

c) $y - x = \boxed{}$

d) $x - y = \boxed{}$

e) $\dfrac{y}{x} = \boxed{}$

f) $\dfrac{x}{y} = \boxed{}$

g) $3x - 2y = \boxed{}$

5 Find the missing terms.

a) $3d - 7d \equiv \boxed{}$

b) $e - 7e + 3e \equiv \boxed{}$

c) $-7f + 3f \equiv \boxed{}$

d) $7g + \boxed{} \equiv 3g$

e) $-7h - \boxed{} \equiv 3h$

f) $7k + 3 + -3k - 4 \equiv \boxed{}$

6   Solve the equations.

a) $-6a = 18$

$a = $ ___

c) $3d + 30 = 9$

$d = $ ___

b) $\dfrac{c}{9} = -8$

$c = $ ___

d) $-5e - 4 = -19$

$e = $ ___

7   Expand the brackets.

a) $6(g - 3) \equiv$ _____

e) $7(x - y) \equiv$ _____

b) $4(7 + m) \equiv$ _____

f) $9(4n - 3q) \equiv$ _____

c) $5(6k + 1) \equiv$ _____

g) $4e(e + 5) \equiv$ _____

d) $8(6h - 4) \equiv$ _____

h) $8p(7u - 2p) \equiv$ _____

8   Fill in the boxes to make the statements correct.

a) $3(\boxed{} + 4) \equiv 15r + \boxed{}$

b) $\boxed{}(3t - 6) \equiv 21t - \boxed{}$

9   Expand the expressions.

a) $-4(b + 8) \equiv$ _____

c) $-6(-3 + 4m) \equiv$ _____

b) $-5(e - 6) \equiv$ _____

d) $-7k(-k - 5) \equiv$ _____

10   Write an expression for the area of each shape.

a)

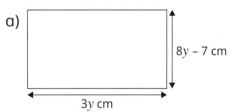

$8y - 7$ cm

$3y$ cm

area = _____

b)

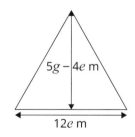

$5g - 4e$ m

$12e$ m

area = _____

Brackets, equations & inequalities

Date:

Let's remember

1. Evaluate the expression $3y - 2$ when $y = -4$

2. **H** A number card is chosen, and a letter card is chosen.

   How many possible outcomes are there?

1	2	3

A	B	C	D

3. Is the sequence 5, 8, 11, 14, ... linear or non-linear? _____

4. Write the ratio $20:300$ in the form $1:n$

   _____

Let's practise

1. List the factors of the numbers or expressions.

   a) 15 _____

   b) 24 _____

   c) $5y$ _____

   d) $3ab$ _____

2. Fill in the boxes and complete the factorisations.

   a)

   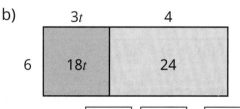

	m	3
4	$4m$	12

   $4m + 12 \equiv 4(\boxed{} + \boxed{})$

   b)

	$3t$	4
6	$18t$	24

   $18t + 24 \equiv \boxed{}(\boxed{} + \boxed{})$

3 Factorise the expressions fully.

a) $5n + 15 \equiv$ _____

b) $8p - 10 \equiv$ _____

c) $12q - 8 \equiv$ _____

d) $20 + 24g \equiv$ _____

e) $45 - 20n \equiv$ _____

f) $42a + 12b \equiv$ _____

g) $7c - 7 \equiv$ _____

h) $16k + 40k^2 \equiv$ _____

4 Simplify the expressions.

a) $4(3m + 6) - 7 \equiv$ _____

b) $8 + 4(3m + 6) \equiv$ _____

c) $4(3m + 6) + 9m \equiv$ _____

d) $6 + 4(3m + 6) - 5m \equiv$ _____

5 a) Expand $4(p + 2)$ _____

b) Expand $3(p + 5)$ _____

c) Use your answers to part a) and part b) to simplify $4(p + 2) + 3(p + 5)$

_____

6 a) Expand $5(3w + 2) \equiv$ _____

b) Expand $4(6w - 1) \equiv$ _____

c) Use your answers to part a) and part b) to simplify $5(3w + 2) + 4(6w - 1)$

_____

7 Expand and simplify the expressions.

a) $5(e + 5) + 3e - 6 \equiv$ _____

b) $6(3g + 5) + 7(2g - 3) \equiv$ _____

c) $5(2k - 4) + 4(k + 3) \equiv$ _____

d) $4(7h - 1) + 8(3h - 4) \equiv$ _____

e) $7(4m + 5) + 6(3 + 2m) \equiv$ _____

f) $7(4m - 5) + 6(3 - 2m) \equiv$ _____

g) $5(3n + 6) - 4(n + 2) \equiv$ _____

h) $5(3n + 6) - 4(n - 2) \equiv$ _____

8   Find the area of the compound shape.

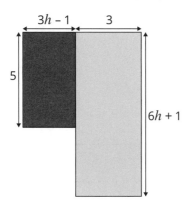

9   Use the algebra tiles to complete the expansion.

H

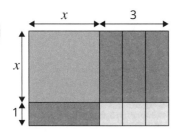

$(x + 3)(x + 1) \equiv$ _____

10   Expand and simplify the expressions.

H

a) $(g + 5)(g + 7) \equiv$ _____

b) $(2m + 3)(m + 4) \equiv$ _____

c) $(p + 5)(3p + 2) \equiv$ _____

11   Use algebra tiles to complete the expansion.

H

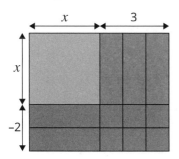

$(x + 3)(x – 2) \equiv$ _____

12   Expand and simplify the expressions.

H

a) $(e + 7)(e – 2) \equiv$ _____

b) $(w – 5)(w – 4) \equiv$ _____

c) $(2h + 3)(h – 5) \equiv$ _____

How did you find these questions?

Very easy   1   2   3   4   5   6   7   8   9   10   Very difficult

Brackets, equations & inequalities

Date:

Let's remember

1   Factorise the expression fully.

   $12g + 30 \equiv$ _____

2   Expand $5(4x - 3) \equiv$ _____

3   Alex asks some people about their favourite season.

Season	Frequency
Spring	38
Summer	53
Autumn	19
Winter	15

   How many people did Alex ask? [   ]

4   8 books cost £17.60

   How much do 5 books cost?   £ [   ]

Let's practise

1   Solve the equations.

   a) $b + 7 = 15$

      $b =$ [   ]

   b) $d - 5 = 4$

      $d =$ [   ]

   c) $-3 = g - 8$

      $g =$ [   ]

   d) $9 - m = 5$

      $m =$ [   ]

   e) $5h = 16$

      $h =$ [   ]

   f) $\frac{w}{4} = -8$

      $w =$ [   ]

   g) $6a = -42$

      $a =$ [   ]

   h) $5 = 10n$

      $n =$ [   ]

2   Solve the equations.

a) $4 = 4c + 8$

$c =$ ⬚

b) $\dfrac{e}{3} - 5 = -7$

$e =$ ⬚

c) $17 - 3f = 5$

$f =$ ⬚

d) $-4 = -k + 9$

$k =$ ⬚

e) $\dfrac{1}{4}v - 5 = 6$

$v =$ ⬚

f) $-6r - 3 = 9$

$r =$ ⬚

3   Solve the equations.

a) $3(y - 8) = 24$

$y =$ ⬚

b) $5(4g + 3) = 25$

$g =$ ⬚

c) $4(7 - 2x) = 20$

$x =$ ⬚

d) $48 = -3(6h - 4)$

$h =$ ⬚

4   Annie has 3 boxes of cupcakes and 5 extra cupcakes.

Each box contains the same number of cupcakes.

There are 23 cupcakes in total.

Form and solve an equation to work out how many cupcakes Annie has in each box.

_____

5   The area of the rectangle is 70 cm²

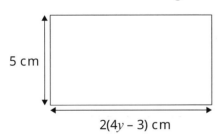

5 cm

2(4y – 3) cm

Work out the value of y and find the perimeter of the rectangle.

$y =$ ⬚   perimeter = ⬚ cm

6 Match the inequalities with the description.

$k < -3$	k is less than or equal to 3
$-3 \leq k$	k is greater than or equal to -3
$-3 < k < 3$	k is greater than -3 and less than 3
$3 \geq k$	k is less than -3

7 Solve the inequalities.

a) $y + 5 < 9$ _____

c) $8 + p \leq 6$ _____

b) $m - 3 \geq 24$ _____

d) $7g < 35$ _____

8 Find all of the integer values that satisfy the inequalities.

a) $-3 < d \leq 4$ _____

b) $-6 \leq 2g < 3$ _____

c) $-1 < h + 4 < 7$ _____

How did you find these questions?

Very easy   1   2   3   4   5   6   7   8   9   10   Very difficult

Brackets, equations & inequalities

Let's remember

1. Solve the equation $5k + 3 = 11$

   $k =$ ☐

2. Expand and simplify $2(3y + 5) + 4(6y - 2)$

   _____

3. A 6-sided fair dice is rolled.

   What is the probability that the score is a prime number? _____

4. The scale on a diagram says that 5 cm represents 1 m.

   What does 15 cm on the diagram represent in real life?

   _____

Let's practise

1. Solve the inequalities.

   a) $6b + 3 < 39$ _____

   c) $12 > 5x - 4$ _____

   b) $4y - 2 \geq 12$ _____

   d) $15 \leq 8 + 6c$ _____

2. Tommy thinks of a number.

   He multiplies it by 5 and then subtracts 6

   His answer is less than 30

   a) Form an inequality for Tommy's number. _____

   b) Solve your inequality to describe the range of possible numbers.

   _____

③ A cup of coffee costs £y

A cup of tea costs £1.50

Mrs Dean buys 4 cups of coffee and 6 cups of tea.

The total is less than £20

a) Form an inequality. _____

b) Solve it to describe the range of possible values of y

_____

c) What is the maximum possible cost of a cup of coffee?

_____

④ Solve the equations.

a) $4w - 3 = w + 12$

$w = \boxed{}$

b) $3x - 6 = 5x - 22$

$x = \boxed{}$

c) $6v + 2 = 3v - 4$

$v = \boxed{}$

d) $8 + 7d = 3d - 8$

$d = \boxed{}$

⑤ Solve the inequalities.

a) $5b + 8 > 3b + 14$ _____

b) $2g + 5 \leq 4g - 4$ _____

c) $3 + 4g < g - 15$ _____

d) $11 + 8k \geq 8 + 5k$ _____

⑥ Match the correct pairs.

$3(y - 2) \equiv 3y - 6$	equation
$3y - 6$	expression
$3y - 6 = 2$	formula
$3y - 6 = x$	identity

7 This is an isosceles triangle.

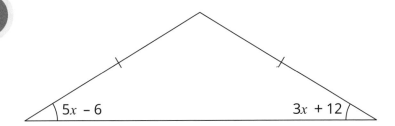

5x – 6   3x + 12

a) Work out the value of x.

$x =$ [ ] $^\circ$

b) Work out the size of the largest angle in the triangle.

largest angle = [ ] $^\circ$

8 The formula for the area of a triangle is half of the base multiplied by the perpendicular height.

a) Write an algebraic formula for the area, A, of a triangle given the base b and perpendicular height h

$A =$ _____

b) Form and solve an equation to find y in this triangle.

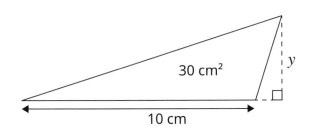

30 cm²

y

10 cm

Diagram not drawn to scale

$y =$ [ ] cm

How did you find these questions?

Very easy   1   2   3   4   5   6   7   8   9   10   Very difficult

Block 2   Sequences

In this block, you extend your knowledge of the sequences you learned at the start of last year, and use maths from other topic areas. You start by looking at **term-to-term rules**. The rule for this sequence is 'start with –2, add 7 each time'.

–2	5	12	19	2	6

You also learn about **position-to-term rules**. The rule for this sequence is 'the **position** multiplied by 4, then add 3'. Position just means the place in the sequence.
Can you see how the rule works?

7	11	15	19	23

You also use tables to help you generate sequences from position-to-term rules, like this sequence, which is for the rule $4n + 5$

n	1	2	3	4	5
$4n$					
$4n + 5$					

You explore sequences of **patterns**. In this block, you learn how to find the rule for sequences like this one.

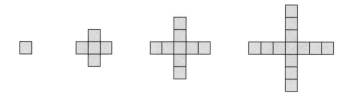

Key vocabulary

Sequence   Position   Term   Linear

Term-to-term rule   Position-to-term rule   Expression

Sequences

Let's remember

1. Solve $3x > 15$ _____

2. Solve $2x + 7 = 25$

   $x =$ ☐

3. Write an expression for 8 less than y _____

4. $3 \times \frac{1}{2} = \dfrac{\square}{\square}$

Let's practise

1. Write the first five terms of each sequence, using the term-to-term rules given.

   a) The 1st term is 7. Add 6 each time.

   _____

   b) The 1st term is 7. Subtract 6 each time.

   _____

   c) The 1st term is 14. Subtract 8 and then double to find the next term.

   _____

2. Describe each of the sequences, using a term-to-term rule.

   a) 16, 11, 6, 1, –4

   _____

   b) –25, –17, –9, –1, 7

   _____

3   Generate the first five terms of each sequence, using the position-to-term rules given.

a) The 7 times-table

_____

b) The –4 times-table

_____

c) 8 more than the 5 times-table

_____

d) 3 less than the 6 times-table

_____

e) The position multiplied by 8, and then add 2

_____

4   Complete the tables to generate sequences from the given rules.

a)

n	1	2	3	4	5
$3n$					

b)

n	1	2	3	4	5
$4n$					
$4n + 5$					

5   Generate the first five terms of the sequences.

a) $5n + 7$ b) $8n - 3$ c) $3n - 8$

_____   _____   _____

6   Complete the table to generate the sequence from the given rule.

n	1	2	3	4	5
$-8n$					
$-8n + 3$					

7 Generate the first five terms of each sequence.

a) $11n - 6$ _____

b) $-11n - 6$ _____

c) $6 - 11n$ _____

d) $2(5n + 1)$ _____

e) $2(1 - 5n)$ _____

8 Write the first five terms of each sequence.

a) $n^2 + 1$ _____

b) $n^3 - 1$ _____

c) $\dfrac{2}{n}$ _____

d) $\dfrac{n - 1}{n}$ _____

9 Complete the table.

H

Sequence	nth term	20th term
8, 17, 26, 35		
	$7n + 12$	
−8, −16, −24, −32		
−1, −7, −13, −19		

10 Here is a sequence of shapes.

H

   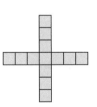

a) What is the rule for the nth term of the sequence?

_____

b) Does the number 241 appear in this sequence? Explain your answer.

_____

_____

How did you find these questions?

Very easy   1   2   3   4   5   6   7   8   9   10   Very difficult

Block 3   Indices

In this block, you learn about **indices**. That just means **powers**, for example 5 **squared** is just 5 multiplied by 5. If you multiply 5 by itself 3 times, then this is 5 **cubed**. The number of times you multiply a number by itself is the power or **index**.

For example, $5 \times 5 \times 5 \times 5 \times 5 \times 5 \times 5 = 5^7$

You simplify **expressions** like this one by adding and subtracting.

$$7m^2 + 6m^2 - 2m^2 =$$

You simplify expressions involving indices like this one by multiplying.

$$5f \times 5f^2 \equiv$$

You simplify expressions like this one involving indices and fractions.

$$\frac{6 \times p2 \times p \times p}{3 \times q} \equiv$$

You also simplify expressions involving indices and division, like this one. By the end of this block, you'll be able to work out the answer.

$$24a^3 b^2 \div 6ab$$

You can also find the power of a power. $(3^2)^4$ is the same as 3^8. Can you see why?

Key vocabulary

Index/Indices   Simplify   Expression   Squared Cubed

Power   Common factor   Exponent

Indices

Let's remember

1. Generate the first five terms of the sequence $3n + 5$

   _____

2. Solve $4g + 3 = 5$

   $g =$ ☐

3. Expand $7(4x - 9)$ _____

4. Work out $4 \div \frac{2}{5}$ ☐

Let's practise

1. Simplify the expressions.

   a) $3y^2 + 4y^2 \equiv$ _____

   b) $9w^2 - 5w^2 \equiv$ _____

   c) $3x^2 + x^2 + 7x^2 \equiv$ _____

   d) $10p^5 - 8p^5 - 3p^5 \equiv$ _____

2. Simplify the expressions, giving your answers as a single term.

   a) $e \times e^2 \times e \times e \equiv$ _____   c) $8k^2 \times 5k \equiv$ _____

   b) $3f \times 4f \equiv$ _____   d) $5u^2 \times 8u \times 3u^2 \equiv$ _____

3. Simplify the expressions.

   a) $h^3 + h^2 + 3h^3 + 2h^2 \equiv$ _____

   b) $5b^3 + b^3 + 2b^2 - b^3 \equiv$ _____

   c) $8p^2 + 5p^3 + 4p^2 - 2p^2 - 4p^3 \equiv$ _____

   d) $7a^3 + a + a^2 - a^3 + 3a \equiv$ _____

4 Simplify the expressions.

a) $x \times x \times y \times x \times y \equiv$ _____

b) $w \times 5 \times v \times w \times 3 \times v \times w \times 4 \equiv$ _____

5 By thinking about their factors, simplify the expressions.

a) $\dfrac{12bc}{4b} \equiv$ _____

b) $\dfrac{20f^2g^3}{5fg} \equiv$ _____

c) $\dfrac{24h^2k^3}{6k^2h} \equiv$ _____

6 Work out the results of the divisions.

a) $36gh \div 9 \equiv$ _____

c) $24km^2 \div 3m \equiv$ _____

b) $36gh \div 9g \equiv$ _____

d) $24km^2 \div 12m^2 \equiv$ _____

7 Simplify the expressions.

a) $5^3 \times 5^6 \equiv$ _____

d) $5g^4 \times 3g^2 \equiv$ _____

b) $c^7 \times c^5 \equiv$ _____

e) $h^3n^2 \times h^4n \times m^5n^3 \equiv$ _____

c) $x^{10} \times x^{20} \times x^{30} \equiv$ _____

8 Simplify the expressions, giving each answer as a single term.

a) $3^{12} \div 3^4 \equiv$ _____

c) $6g^9 \div g^3 \equiv$ _____

b) $h^8 \div h^2 \equiv$ _____

d) $7p^4n^5 \div 2p^4n^3 \equiv$ _____

9 Simplify the expressions.

H

a) $(x^3)^2 \equiv$ _____

c) $(4m)^2 \equiv$ _____

b) $(y^{12})^3 \equiv$ _____

d) $(3g^5)^2 \equiv$ _____

10 Simplify the expressions.

H

a) $(m^3)^2 \times m^5 \equiv$ _____

c) $(w^8 \div w^5)^3 \equiv$ _____

b) $(a^3 \times a^7)^4 \equiv$ _____

d) $((y^3)^4)^5 \equiv$ _____

How did you find these questions?

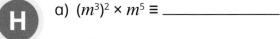

Very easy   1   2   3   4   5   6   7   8   9   10   Very difficult

Block 4 Fractions & percentages

In this block, you build on your knowledge of **fractions** and **percentages**. You need to know how fractions, **decimals** and percentages are **equivalent**. As fractions, A and B are $\frac{1}{5}$ and $\frac{13}{20}$, as shown on this number line. Can you see what they are as percentages?

You will sometimes need to work with **percentages** over 100%.
125% is equivalent to the decimal 1.25
Can you see why?

You can use bar models to help you to work out **percentage changes**. The bar model on the left shows a 20% **decrease**. Do you know what percentage change the bar model on the right shows?

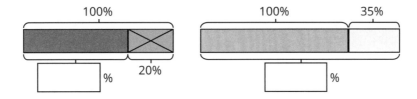

You solve percentage problems to do with money. If Rosie has £120 and she spends £78, what percentage of her money does she have left?

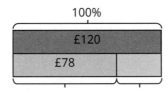

You also solve reverse percentage problems. Max got 63 marks in a test, and a score of 70%. How many marks were there in the test?

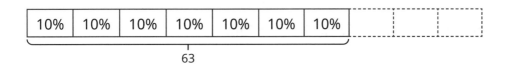

Key vocabulary

Percentage   Fraction   Decimal   Percentage change

Decrease   Increase   Equivalent   Original   Profit   Multiplier   Loss

Fractions & percentages

Date:

Let's remember

1   Simplify $3y^2 \times 2y^3 \times 2y^2$

_____

2   Write the first five terms of the sequence $4n + 1$

_____

3   Solve the inequality $3x + 7 > 31$

_____

4   Write the coordinates of three points that lie on the line $y = 2x$

_____

Let's practise

1   a) Write the percentages, decimals and fractions indicated by the arrows.

A = $\boxed{}$ % = $\boxed{}$ = $\dfrac{\boxed{}}{100}$ = $\dfrac{\boxed{}}{5}$

B = $\boxed{}$ % = $\boxed{}$ = $\dfrac{\boxed{}}{100}$ = $\dfrac{\boxed{}}{20}$

b) Label 80% and 0.35 on the number line.

c) i) Write 80% as a decimal and a fraction.

    _____

   ii) Write 0.35 as a percentage and a fraction.

    _____

2   Convert the percentages to decimals.

   a) 53% = [   ]

   b) 31% = [   ]

   c) 30% = [   ]

   d) 3% = [   ]

3   Convert the decimals to percentages.

   a) 0.19 = _____

   b) 0.99 = _____

   c) 0.09 = _____

   d) 0.9 = _____

4   Convert the fractions to percentages.

   a) $\dfrac{41}{100}$ = _____

   b) $\dfrac{14}{100}$ = _____

   c) $\dfrac{41}{50}$ = _____

   d) $\dfrac{1}{4}$ = _____

5   Work these out without using a calculator. Show how you worked out your answers.

   a) 20% of 80 = [   ]

   b) 75% of 60 cm = [   ] cm

   c) $\dfrac{1}{5}$ of 70 kg = [   ] kg

   d) $\dfrac{7}{10}$ of £2000 = £ [   ]

6   Use a calculator to work out the amounts.

   a) 59% of 3000 = _____

   b) 17% of £2900 = _____

   c) 82.3% of 680 m = _____

   d) $\dfrac{2}{3}$ of 816 = _____

   e) $\dfrac{4}{5}$ of 1650 kg = _____

   f) $\dfrac{7}{9}$ of 6741 = _____

7   A local bakery invests £5400 in a bank account.

   The bakery receives 2.35% annual interest on their investment.

   Work out how much interest the bakery makes in 1 year. _____

8   a) Write the percentages, decimals and fractions indicated by the arrows.

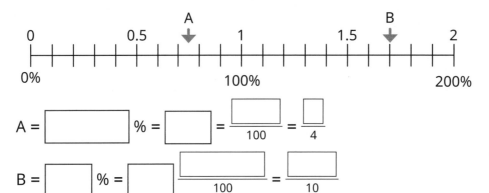

A = [＿＿＿＿] % = [＿＿＿] = $\dfrac{\boxed{}}{100}$ = $\dfrac{\boxed{}}{4}$

B = [＿＿＿] % = [＿＿＿] $\dfrac{\boxed{}}{100}$ = $\dfrac{\boxed{}}{10}$

b) Label 120% and 1.55 on the number line.

c) i) Write 120% as a decimal and as a fraction in its simplest form.

_____

ii) Write 1.55 as a percentage and as a fraction in its simplest form.

_____

9   Complete the table.

Percentage	Decimal
100%	
103%	
	1.25
	1.09
230%	
	2.57

10   Write the values in ascending order.

a) $\dfrac{2}{5}$ 25%   0.52   2.5

_____

b) 1.09   19% $\dfrac{1}{9}$ 1.9

_____

How did you find these questions?

Very easy   1   2   3   4   5   6   7   8   9   10   Very difficult

Fractions & percentages

Date:

Let's remember

1 Convert 80% to a decimal.

2 Simplify $a^3b^5 \times a^2b^7 \equiv$ _____

3 Solve $3x + 1 \leq 7$

_____

4 For every 5 pens in a tub there are 7 pencils.

There are 35 pens.

How many pencils are there?

Let's practise

1 Match the decreases to the percentage remaining and the corresponding decimal.

The first one has been done for you.

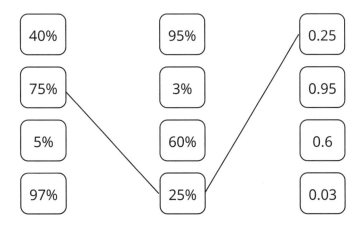

40%		95%		0.25
75%		3%		0.95
5%		60%		0.6
97%		25%		0.03

2 Work out the missing percentages.

a)
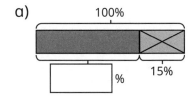

100%

15%

%

b)
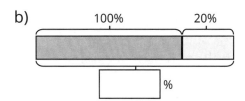

100%   20%

%

c) Convert the percentages to decimals.

  i) 65% =

  ii) 165% =

  iii) 160% =

  iv) 106% =

69

3 a) Write the decimal multiplier you would use to work out the increases and decreases.

i)   Increase by 30% = [   ]   iv) Decrease by 17% = [   ]

ii) Decrease by 30% = [   ]   v) Increase by 1% = [   ]

iii) Increase by 17% = [   ]   vi) Decrease by 1% = [   ]

b) Complete the calculations.

i)   Increase £60 by 30% = £ [   ]

ii) Decrease £60 by 17% = £ [   ]

iii) Increase £60 by 1% = £ [   ]

4 a) The price of a laptop is £560

In a sale the price is decreased by 35%

Work out the price of the laptop in the sale. £ [   ]

b) In 2021, the value of a house was £250 000

In 2022, the value of the house increased by 17%

What was the value of the house in 2022? £ [   ]

c) A car garage invests £15 000 in a bank account. The garage receives 1.7% annual interest on their investment.

Work out the value of the investment after 1 year. £ [   ]

5 Complete the conversions.

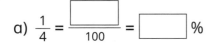

a) $\dfrac{1}{4} = \dfrac{\boxed{}}{100} = \boxed{}$ %

b) $\dfrac{4}{5} = \dfrac{\boxed{}}{100} = \boxed{}$ %

c) $\dfrac{11}{20} = \dfrac{\boxed{}}{100} = \boxed{}$ %

d) $\dfrac{74}{200} = \dfrac{\boxed{}}{100} = \boxed{}$ %

6 Mo scored 46 out of 50 on a maths test.

a) Complete the working to show his test mark as a percentage.

$$\frac{46}{50} = \frac{\boxed{}}{100} = \boxed{}\,\%$$

b) Mo scored 24 out of 30 on a science test.

Complete the working to show his test mark as a percentage.

$$\frac{24}{30} = \frac{\boxed{}}{10} = \frac{\boxed{}}{100} = \boxed{}\,\%$$

c) Whitney scored 36 out of 50 on the maths test.
She scored 21 out of 30 on the science test.

In which test did Whitney score a higher percentage?

_____

7 There are 13 apples and 15 pears in a bag of fruit.

a) What fraction of the fruit are apples?

b) What percentage of the fruit are apples? Give your answer to 1 decimal place.

_____

8 The price of a coat is increased by 20%. A week later, there is a sale and the price of the coat is reduced by 20%. Is the price of the coat now higher or lower, or the same as it was before the sale?

_____

9 Express the first quantity as a fraction and a percentage of the second quantity. Give your percentages to the nearest whole %.

a) 756 grams, 3 kg _____

c) 7 minutes, 1 hour _____

b) 79 cm, 5 metres _____

d) 6 days, 2 weeks _____

How did you find these questions?

Very easy   1   2   3   4   5   6   7   8   9   10   Very difficult

Fractions & percentages

Date:

Let's remember

1 Write the decimal multiplier you would use to increase an amount by 12% _____

2 Work out 35% of £60   £ [   ]

3 Describe the sequence 15, 13, 11, 9, 7 using a term-to-term rule.

_____

4 Find the midpoint of the line segment with (0, 0) and (6, 10) as endpoints.

_____

Let's practise

1 Rosie has £50

She spends £28

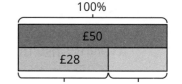

a) What fraction of her money does she spend? _____

b) What percentage of her money does she spend? _____

c) What percentage of her money does she have left? _____

2 Dora buys a book for £10

Later, she sells it for £14

a) Does Dora make a profit or a loss? _____

b) How much profit or loss does she make?   £ [   ]

c) Circle the fraction that is the most useful to work out Dora's percentage profit or loss.

$\dfrac{10}{14}$ $\dfrac{4}{10}$ $\dfrac{4}{14}$ $\dfrac{14}{10}$

d) What percentage profit or loss does she make? _____

3 Esther earns £250 a month. She gets a pay rise and now earns £300 a month.

a) How much extra does Esther earn per month?   £ [   ]

b) What is her percentage pay rise? _____

4 A hotel company buys a house for £302 000

The company later sells the house for £319 950

a) How much profit does the company make from the sale?   £ [   ]

b) Calculate the percentage profit that the company makes.

Give your answer to 2 decimal places.

[   ]

5 A school has 1235 students.

20% of the students are in Year 8

a) How many students are in Year 8?

[   ]

b) 758 of the students in the school have a pet.

What percentage of the students in the school don't have a pet?

Give your answer to 1 decimal place.

[   ]

6 The population of a country increases from 67.33 million to 68.76 million.

Work out the percentage increase in population.

Give your answer correct to 1 decimal place.

[   ]

7 Olivia answers 70% of the questions on a test correctly.

H She scores 63 marks.

| 10% | 10% | 10% | 10% | 10% | 10% | 10% | | | |

£63

How many marks are there on the test? [   ]

8 In a sale, normal prices are reduced by 20%. Ron bought a pair of trainers in the sale.

H The sale price of the trainers was £48

Calculate the normal price of the trainers. £ ☐

9 Tommy buys 20 chocolate bars. He pays £12 for the chocolate bars.

H Tommy sells each chocolate bar for 75 pence.

Work out Tommy's percentage profit.

☐

10 a) Last month, Ms Fisher received a 5% pay rise. She now earns £1732.50 a month.

H How much did she earn before the pay rise? £ ☐

b) Mrs Dean received a 2.5% pay rise. Her wage increased by £65 a month.

What is her yearly wage after the increase? £ ☐

11 A shop normally sells their items at 65% above cost price.

H In a sale, the shop reduces the prices by 15%.

What percentage profit does the shop make on items sold in the sale?

☐

12 The area of the triangle is 32% greater than the area of the rectangle.

H Work out the height of the triangle.

$h =$ ☐

15 cm

7 cm

h

12 cm

Diagram not drawn to scale

How did you find these questions?

Very easy   1   2   3   4   5   6   7   8   9   10   Very difficult

Block 5 Standard index form

In this block, you learn about **standard index form**, which you can also say as just **standard form**. It is used for very large or very small numbers, to make them easier to understand. Here is an example of a standard form number. It means 8 000 000 000, or 8 billion!

$$8 \times 10^9$$

You can also use standard form for very small numbers. Did you know, a water molecule is about 2.7×10^{-10} metres across. That's 0.00000000027

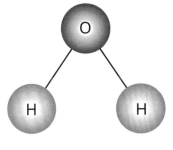

Standard form makes it easier to compare and order small and large numbers. This list is in ascending order. Can you see why?

4.3×10^{-2}

3.4×10^4

3.04×10^5

3.04×10^6

You calculate in standard form. Here's an example of a calculation using standard form.

$$(3.2 \times 10^4)(4.8 \times 10^2) = 1.536 \times 10^3$$

You need to be careful when adding and subtracting in standard form. Can you see why this calculation is correct?

$$3 \times 10^4 + 2 \times 10^5 = 2.3 \times 10^5$$

You also solve problems in standard form. If there are approximately 5×10^9 red blood cells per millilitre of blood, approximately how many red blood cells are there in 10 pints of blood?

Key vocabulary

Base Index/Indices Standard-index-form Place value

Power (of 10) Exponent

Standard index form

Date:

Let's remember

1   Write 15 as a percentage of 120

2   Ron got 17 out of 20 marks on a test. Write this score as a percentage.

3   Factorise $3x + 9$ _____

4   What type of correlation is shown?

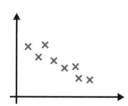

Let's practise

1   Match the numbers with the same value.

10^3	1000
10^7	10
10^1	10 000
10^4	10 000 000

2   Write the numbers in ascending order.

    1 million 10^5 ten thousand 10^{15} 10 000 000

_____

3 Complete the statements.

a) $4000 = 4 \times \boxed{} = 4 \times 10^3$

b) $700 = 7 \times \boxed{} = \boxed{} \times 10^{\boxed{}}$

c) $3\,000\,000 = 3 \times \boxed{} = \boxed{} \times 10^{\boxed{}}$

d) two hundred thousand $= \boxed{} \times \boxed{} = \boxed{} \times 10^{\boxed{}}$

e) eight billion $= \boxed{} \times \boxed{} = \boxed{} \times 10^{\boxed{}}$

f) six million $= \boxed{} \times \boxed{} = \boxed{} \times 10^{\boxed{}}$

4 Tick the numbers that are written correctly in standard index form.

70×10^2 2×10^7 0.7×10^2 7×10^0

$2 \times 10^{0.7}$ 1×10^{100} $2 \times 10^{\frac{7}{10}}$ $\frac{1}{6}$

5 Write the standard form numbers as ordinary numbers.

a) $5 \times 10^4 = $ _____

b) $9 \times 10^6 = $ _____

c) $4 \times 10^7 = $ _____

d) $3 \times 10^9 = $ _____

6 Write the numbers in standard index form.

a) $30\,000 = $ _____

b) $370\,000 = $ _____

c) $37\,500 = $ _____

d) $3\,050\,000 = $ _____

e) $0.0008 = $ _____

f) $0.000083 = $ _____

g) $0.00000836 = $ _____

h) $0.00803 = $ _____

7 Write the standard form numbers as ordinary numbers.

a) $8 \times 10^6 = $ _____

b) $8.3 \times 10^6 = $ _____

c) $8.03 \times 10^6 = $ _____

d) $8.003 \times 10^6 = $ _____

e) $7.51 \times 10^5 = $ _____

f) $7.0051 \times 10^5 = $ _____

8 a) The planet Mercury has an approximate radius of 2.44 million metres.

Write this length in standard form. _____

b) The planet Jupiter has an approximate radius of 7.15×10^7 metres.

Write this length using an ordinary number. [   ] m

9 Match the numbers with the same value.

10^{-1}	$\dfrac{1}{10000}$	0.01
10^{-4}	$\dfrac{1}{10}$	0.0001
10^{-2}	$\dfrac{1}{1000000}$	0.1
10^{-6}	$\dfrac{1}{100}$	0.000001

10 Write the standard form numbers as ordinary numbers.

a) $4 \times 10^{-5} =$ [   ]   c) $6 \times 10^{-7} =$ [   ]

b) $8 \times 10^{-4} =$ [   ]   d) $9 \times 10^{-8} =$ [   ]

11 a) A skin cell is about 0.00002 metres wide.

Write this length in standard form. _____

b) A water molecule is about, 2.7×10^{-10} m long.

Write this length using an ordinary number. [   ] m

12 Write the numbers in ascending order.

a) 2.6×10^7 2.5×10^8 2.58×10^7 2×10^9

_____

b) 3.9×10^{-3} 3.9×10^3 3.09×10^{-3} 3.91×10^{-3}

_____

How did you find these questions?

Very easy   1   2   3   4   5   6   7   8   9   10   Very difficult

Standard index form

Let's remember

1 Write 10^4 as an ordinary number. _____

2 A laptop is priced at £450. The laptop is reduced by 30% in a sale.

   Work out the sale price of the laptop.   £ [＿＿＿＿＿]

3 Use a calculator to work out 15.7% of £3500   £ [＿＿＿＿＿]

4 $\frac{5}{6} \times \frac{1}{2} =$ [＿＿＿]

Let's practise

1 Complete the calculations. Give your answers in standard form.

   a) $(6 \times 10^5) \times 10 =$ _____

   b) $(6 \times 10^5) \times 100 =$ _____

   c) $(6 \times 10^5) \div 1000 =$ _____

   d) $(2.7 \times 10^{-4}) \times 10 =$ _____

   e) $(2.7 \times 10^{-4}) \div 100 =$ _____

   f) $(2.7 \times 10^{-4}) \times 1000 =$ _____

2 Complete the calculations. Give your answers in standard form.

   a) $2 \times (4 \times 10^6) =$ _____

   b) $3.7 \times (2 \times 10^6) =$ _____

   c) $3 \times (3.01 \times 10^{-4}) =$ _____

   d) $2 \times 2 \times (2.1 \times 10^{-2}) =$ _____

3 These numbers are not in correct standard form. Convert them to standard form.

a) $30 \times 10^4 = $ _____

e) $0.6 \times 10^7 = $ _____

b) $4000 \times 10^6 = $ _____

f) $350 \times 10^{-4} = $ _____

c) $700 \times 10^{-5} = $ _____

g) $0.091 \times 10^5 = $ _____

d) $82 \times 10^3 = $ _____

h) $0.0021 \times 10^{-2} = $ _____

4 Complete the calculations. Give your answers in standard form.

a) $(6 \times 10^9) \div 3 = $ _____

b) $(6.9 \times 10^9) \div 3 = $ _____

c) $(8 \times 10^{-4}) \div 2 = $ _____

d) $4 \times (6 \times 10^{-3}) \div 3 = $ _____

5 Complete the calculations. Give your answers in standard form.

a) $(7 \times 10^5) + (2 \times 10^5) = $ _____

b) $(2 \times 10^{-3}) + (6 \times 10^{-3}) = $ _____

c) $(5 \times 10^6) + 10^6 = $ _____

d) $(7 \times 10^5) - (2 \times 10^5) = $ _____

e) $(3.4 \times 10^4) + (2.7 \times 10^4) = $ _____

f) $(5.3 \times 10^{-3}) - (2.9 \times 10^{-3}) = $ _____

6 Tommy is adding numbers in standard form.

He writes $(7 \times 10^4) + (5 \times 10^4) = 12 \times 10^4$

Explain the mistake that Tommy has made.

_____

7 Work out the calculations. Give your answers in standard form.

a) $(3.5 \times 10^3) + (2.9 \times 10^4)$

c) $(3.5 \times 10^{-3}) + (7.9 \times 10^{-2})$

_____   _____

b) $(7.8 \times 10^5) - (9.2 \times 10^4)$

d) $(4.1 \times 10^{-5}) + (3.6 \times 10^{-6})$

_____   _____

8   Work out the multiplications. Give your answers in standard form.

a) $(2 \times 10^4) \times (3 \times 10^5)$

c) $(2 \times 10^4) \times (8 \times 10^5)$

_____

_____

b) $(3.6 \times 10^{-2}) \times (2 \times 10^3)$

d) $(4.7 \times 10^{-2}) \times (3 \times 10^3)$

_____

_____

9   Work out the divisions. Give your answers in standard form.

a) $(6 \times 10^7) \div (3 \times 10^5)$

c) $(3 \times 10^4) \div (6 \times 10^5)$

_____

_____

b) $(5.8 \times 10^{-2}) \div (2 \times 10^3)$

d) $(4.5 \times 10^2) \div (6 \times 10^{-3})$

_____

_____

10   There are approximately 5×10^9 red blood cells per millilitre of blood.

An average human has a blood volume that is approximately 10 pints.

One pint is equal to 568 ml.

If a person donates 10% of their blood, approximately how many red blood cells have they still got?

Give your answer in standard form to 2 decimal places.

_____

11   Work out the values of the expressions. Give your answers as simplified fractions.

a) $8^{-2} =$ _____

b) $5^{-3} =$ _____

How did you find these questions?

Very easy   1   2   3   4   5   6   7   8   9   10   Very difficult

Block 6   Number sense

In this block, you consolidate a lot of the skills you have learned with number, including **rounding** as shown in this table. You might be able to complete this table with what you already know.

Number	Rounded to 1 decimal place	Rounded to 2 decimal places	Rounded to 3 decimal places
0.38954			
5.0643			
84.6394			
10009.9923			

You **estimate** answers to **calculations**. Look at this example. Can you see that it is a good estimate for the actual answer? The squiggly equals sign just means it is **approximately** correct.

$$\frac{58^2}{241 - 119.2} \approx 30$$

You also **convert units**. Do you know how many grams are in 3.2 kilograms? Dexter thinks it is 3200. Is he correct?

$$3.2 \times 1000 = 3200$$

You solve problems like this one: *'The perimeter of a rectangle is 206 mm. The length of the rectangle is 5.6 cm. Work out the width of the rectangle.'*
Can you work out the answer?

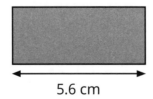

5.6 cm

Key vocabulary

Round   Estimate   Significant figures   Decimal places   Integer

Calculation   Unit   Convert   Approximate

Number sense

Let's remember

1   Write 5 000 000 in standard form. _____

2   Write 4×10^{-4} as an ordinary number. _____

3   Write 15 out of 17 as a percentage. Give your answer to 1 decimal place.

[   ]

4   1 kg is approximately equal to 2.2 lbs.

6 kg ≈ [   ] lbs

Let's practise

1   Complete the sentences.

a) 6793 rounded to the nearest 100 is _____

b) 67 930 rounded to the nearest 10 000 is _____

c) 679.24 rounded to the nearest 10 is _____

d) 210 938 rounded to the nearest 100 is _____

e) 5 000 839 rounded to the nearest 1000 is _____

f) 5 000 839 rounded to the nearest 10 is _____

2   Round the numbers to 1 significant figure.

a) 6.92   [   ]   e) 0.00289   [   ]

b) 29.6   [   ]   f) 0.298   [   ]

c) 962   [   ]   g) 2.0809   [   ]

d) 926 000   [   ]   h) 82 009   [   ]

3   Complete the table.

Number	Rounded to 1 decimal place	Rounded to 2 decimal places	Rounded to 3 decimal places
0.38954			
5.0643			
84.6394			
10 009.9923			

4   A number rounds to 9.8 to 1 decimal place.

The same number rounds to 10 to the nearest integer.

Write three numbers that it could be.

9.6   9.7   9.8   9.9   10   10.1

_____

5   a) Estimate the answers to the calculations. Show your workings.

   i)   28 × 992 ≈ _____

   ii) 23.8 × 29 ≈ _____

   iii) 2382 ÷ 5.3 ≈ _____

   iv) 2382 ÷ 530 ≈ _____

   b) Work out estimates for the answers to the calculations.

   i) $\dfrac{53 \times 28}{84.24 + 18.9}$ ≈ _____

   ii) $\dfrac{78^2}{345 - 95.2}$ ≈ _____

   iii) $\dfrac{24 + 63.28}{1.92^3}$ ≈ _____

   iv) $\dfrac{985 + 832}{0.491}$ ≈ _____

6 Add brackets to make each statement correct.

You may need more than one set of brackets for some statements.

a) i) $6 + 3 \times 8 + 4 = 42$

   ii) $6 + 3 \times 8 + 4 = 108$

b) i) $9 + 5^2 - 7 \times 2 = 45$

   ii) $9 + 5^2 - 7 \times 2 = 54$

7 A pack of 15 bread rolls costs £3.45

A pack of 4 bread rolls costs 99p.

Which pack gives the better value for money?

_____

8 The perimeter of a rectangle is 206 mm.

The length of the rectangle is 5.6 cm.

Work out the width of the rectangle. _____

9 Complete the conversions.

a) 7 kg = [ ] g

b) 1300 g = [ ] kg

c) 2070 ml = [ ] l

d) 13 g = [ ] kg

e) 720 cl = [ ] l

f) 0.04 l = [ ] ml

10 a) A film starts at 6:45 pm.

The film is 2 hours and 17 minutes long.

At what time does the film finish? _____

b) A different film finishes at 8:30 pm.

This film is 95 minutes long.

At what time does this film start? _____

How did you find these questions?

Very easy   1   2   3   4   5   6   7   8   9   10   Very difficult

Time to reflect

Look back through the work you have done this term. Think about what you enjoyed and what you found easy or hard. Talk about this to your teacher and someone at home.

Try these questions	How do you feel about this topic? Tick the box.
The area of the rectangle is 60 cm². By writing and solving an equation, work out the value of x 3(2x –1) cm Area = 60 cm² 4 cm $x =$ ⬜ cm If you need a reminder, look back at brackets, equations & inequalities on pages 45–57	⬜ I am confident and could teach someone else. ⬜ I think I understand but I need practice. ⬜ I don't understand and need help.
Grace scores 84 marks in her English test. Her teacher tells her that this means she got 75%. How many marks were there in total in Grace's test? You can use the bar model to help. ? 25% 25% 25% 25% 84 marks total marks = ⬜ If you need a reminder, look back at fractions & percentages on pages 65–74	⬜ I am confident and could teach someone else. ⬜ I think I understand but I need practice. ⬜ I don't understand and need help.
Work out these calculations, giving your answers in standard form. a) $(4 \times 10^5) + (2.8 \times 10^5) =$ _____ b) $(6 \times 10^4) - (9 \times 10^3) =$ _____ c) $(7.2 \times 10^{-7}) \div (3.6 \times 10^{-5}) =$ _____ If you need a reminder, look back at standard index form on pages 75–81	⬜ I am confident and could teach someone else. ⬜ I think I understand but I need practice. ⬜ I don't understand and need help.

Block 1   Angles in parallel lines & polygons

In this block, you build on the work you did last year on **angles**. You explore angles in **parallel lines** and also in **polygons** – that just means closed shapes with straight sides. You need to be familiar with some new maths terms, like in this diagram where 56° and d are **corresponding angles**.

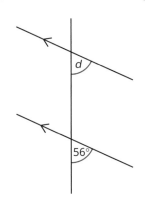

You use your algebra skills to find unknown angles in parallel lines. Here, EF is a **transversal**, and the two shaded angles are **vertically opposite**.

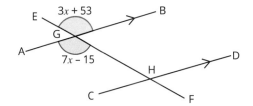

You revisit work you did last year on **constructing** shapes, especially triangles and **quadrilaterals**. To construct a shape like this **equilateral triangle**, you need to use **compasses**.

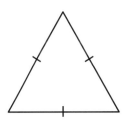

You also explore angles in **regular polygons**. This polygon is a regular **dodecagon**. That means it has 12 sides, and they are all equal length and it has equal angles.

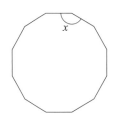

Shapes have **interior** and **exterior** angles. The exterior angles of a shape always sum to 360°. You can use the sum of exterior angles and the sum of interior angles to solve problems. This pentagon has exterior angles of 72° and interior angles of 108°. Can you see why?

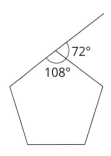

Key vocabulary

Angle   Parallel lines   Polygon   Corresponding angles

Transversal   Vertically opposite   Construct   Quadrilateral   Compasses

Alternate angles   Equilateral triangle   Regular/Irregular polygon

Dodecagon   Protractor   Interior   Exterior

Angles in parallel lines & polygons

Date:

Let's remember

1 Round 8638 to 1 significant figure. ☐

2 Write eight thousand in standard form. _____

3 Increase £60 by 20% £ ☐

4 Expand 4(7k – 2) _____

Let's practise

1 Work out the sizes of the unknown angles. Give reasons for your answers.

a)

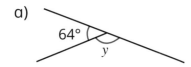

$y =$ ☐ °

_____

_____

b)

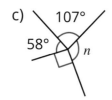

$h =$ ☐ °

_____

_____

c)

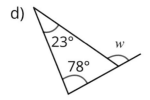

$n =$ ☐ °

_____

_____

d)

$w =$ ☐ °

_____

_____

88

2   Work out the size of the unknown angles.

a)

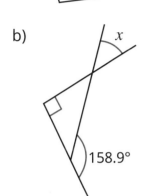

$w =$ [   ] °

b)

$x =$ [   ] °

3   Work out the sizes of the unknown angles. *(Diagrams are not drawn to scale.)*

a)

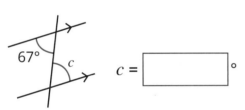

$c =$ [   ] °

c)

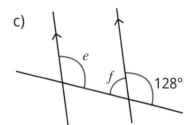

$e =$ [   ] °

$f =$ [   ] °

b)

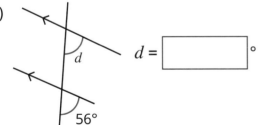

$d =$ [   ] °

d)

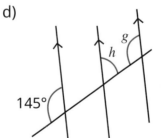

$g =$ [   ] °

$h =$ [   ] °

4   The angles in a triangle are in the ratio 3 : 8 : 7

Is the triangle a right-angled triangle? Explain your answer.

_____

_____

5 Calculate the value of x and y

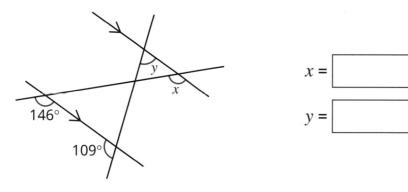

$x =$ [   ] $^\circ$

$y =$ [   ] $^\circ$

6 AB and CD are straight lines. Calculate the value of x

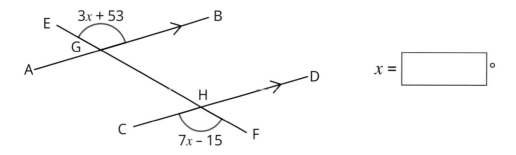

$x =$ [   ] $^\circ$

7 a) Work out the size of $\angle ABC$

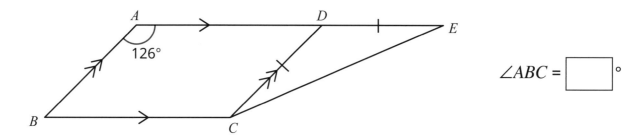

$\angle ABC =$ [   ] $^\circ$

b) Given that ADE is a straight line, calculate the size of $\angle CED$

$\angle CED =$ [   ] $^\circ$

How did you find these questions?

Very easy   1   2   3   4   5   6   7   8   9   10   Very difficult

Angles in parallel lines & polygons

Date:

Let's remember

1 Work out the value of a

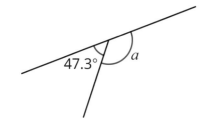

$a = $ ⬚ °

2 Round 34.2901 to 1 decimal place. _____

3 Write 3.2×10^5 as an ordinary number. ⬚

4 Fully factorise the expression $16g + 48$ _____

Let's practise

1 Use a ruler and protractor to make an accurate drawing of triangle ABC.

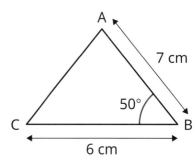

7 cm

50°

C

6 cm

B

A

Diagram not drawn to scale

2 Use a ruler and protractor to make an accurate drawing of triangle DEF.

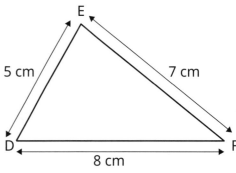

E

5 cm

7 cm

D

8 cm

F

Diagram not drawn to scale

3   Use a ruler and protractor to make an accurate drawing of triangle GHI.

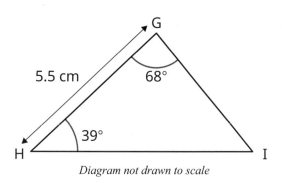

Diagram not drawn to scale

4   Use a ruler and protractor to make an accurate drawing of the trapezium.

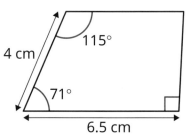

Diagram not drawn to scale

5   a) Here is a parallelogram. Find the unknown sides a and b and angles q, r and s

$a =$ _____

$b =$ _____

$q =$ [   ] °

$r =$ [   ] °

$s =$ [   ] °

b) Here is a rhombus. Find the unknown side e and angle f

$e =$ _____

$f =$ [   ] °

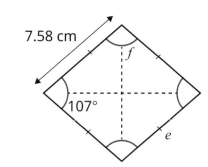

6   The perimeter of the rhombus and parallelogram are the same. Work out the length of x

$x =$ _____

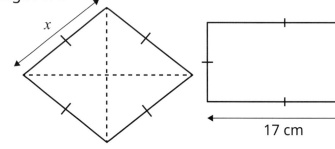

92

7 WXYZ is a kite.

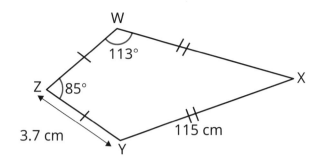

   a) Write the length of side

      i) WZ = [   ] cm

      ii) WX = [   ] cm

   b) What is the size of angle XYZ? [   ] °

   c) Calculate the size of angle WXY. [   ] °

H d) Do the diagonals of this shape intersect at right angles? _____

8 Work out the sizes of the unknown angles.

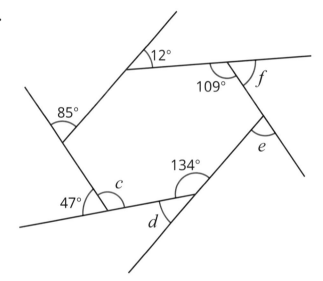

   c = [   ] °

   d = [   ] °

   e = [   ] °

   f = [   ] °

9 What is the sum of the exterior angles of a polygon? [   ] °

10 A regular polygon has nine sides.

   What is the exterior angle of the polygon? [   ] °

How did you find these questions?

Very easy   1   2   3   4   5   6   7   8   9   10   Very difficult

Angles in parallel lines & polygons

Date:

Let's remember

1. How many pairs of parallel sides does a rectangle have? [ ]

2. Work out the value of x.

   Give a reason for your answer.

   _____

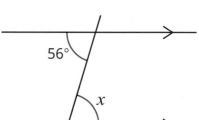

56°

x

3. Write 4×10^{-1} as an ordinary number. [ ]

4. Solve $3x - 1 = 26$

   $x =$ [ ]

Let's practise

1. Work out the sum of the interior angles for each polygon.

   Then work out the sizes of the unknown angles.

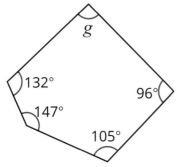

g

132°

96°

147°

105°

   a) Sum of interior angles = [ ]

   $g =$ [ ]

   b)

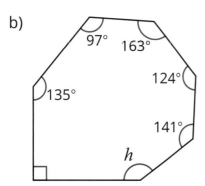

97°   163°

124°

135°

141°

h

   Sum of interior angles = [ ]

   $h =$ [ ]

c)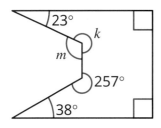

Sum of interior angles = [   ]

$k =$ [   ]

$m =$ [   ]

d)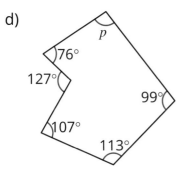

Sum of interior angles = [   ]

$p =$ [   ]

2   The diagram shows a regular dodecagon.

Work out the size of the interior angle x

$x =$ [   ] °

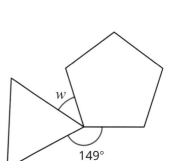

3   A regular polygon has 15 sides.

a) Work out the size of each interior angle. [   ] °

b) Work out the size of each exterior angle. [   ] °

4   a) The diagram shows an equilateral triangle and a regular pentagon.

Find the angle labelled w $w =$ [   ] °

b) The diagram shows two regular polygons.

Find the angle labelled y

$y =$ [   ] °

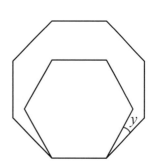

5   For a particular regular polygon, the ratio of the exterior angle to the interior angle is 2:7

Calculate the number of sides that the regular polygon has.

6   AC is a straight line. Show that angle BAC is 30°

H   Explain your reasoning.

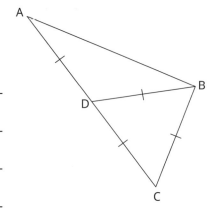

_____

_____

_____

_____

_____

7   a) Use a ruler and pair of compasses to construct the angle bisector of each angle.

H
   i) 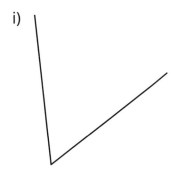   ii)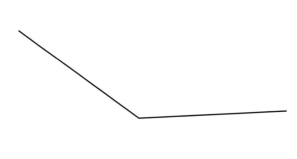

   b) Construct the perpendicular bisector of the line.

How did you find these questions?

Very easy   1   2   3   4   5   6   7   8   9   10   Very difficult

In this block, you build on your knowledge of **area**, and extend it to other shapes. You start by revising what you learned previously about area, for example with these **rectangles** and **parallelograms**. Can you remember the **formulae** for working out their area? What about the formula for the area of a **triangle**?

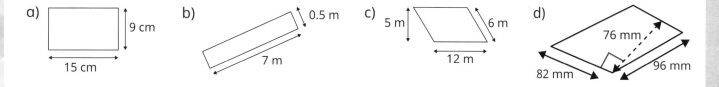

a) 9 cm 15 cm

b) 0.5 m 7 m

c) 5 m 6 m 12 m

d) 76 mm 82 mm 96 mm

You learn about the area of a **trapezium** – that is a kind of **quadrilateral** with a single pair of parallel sides. Here are two examples – watch out though! In trapezium B, one of the lengths isn't actually needed to work out the area.

A 3 cm 8 cm 11 cm

B 17.3 m 12 m 8.5 m 14 m

You investigate the area of a circle. To do this, you need to know that the **radius** of a circle is the distance from the centre to the edge of the circle. Can you see what the radius is here?

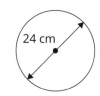

24 cm

You will use π (**Pi**) to calculate the area of a circle. π is a number that can't be written exactly. If you don't have a calculator you can leave your answer in terms of π

You also solve area problems involving **compound shapes**. This shape is a quarter circle on top of a rectangle. Can you see what the height of the rectangle is?

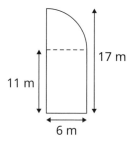

17 m 11 m 6 m

Key vocabulary

Area   Rectangle   Triangle   Parallelogram   Formula   Formulae

Trapezium   Quadrilateral   Circle   Radius   Diameter   Pi   Compound shape

Area of trapezia & circles

Date:

Let's remember

1   Three of the angles in a quadrilateral are 90°, 90° and 104°.

What is the size of the fourth angle? ☐ °

2   What is the sum of the interior angles of a pentagon? ☐ °

3   Estimate the answer to 23 × 59 ☐

4   Write an expression for 5 lots of p _____

Let's practise

1   Find the area of each triangle.

a)

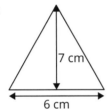

☐ cm²

c)   3 cm

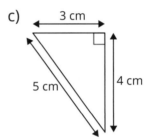

☐ cm²

b)

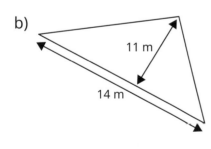

☐ m²

d)   9 mm

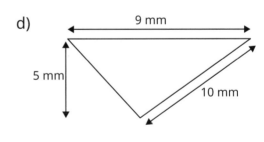

☐ mm²

2   Find the areas of the rectangles and parallelograms.

a)

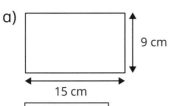

15 cm

9 cm

 cm²

b)

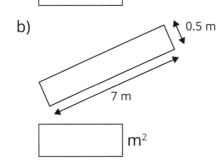

0.5 m

7 m

 m²

c)

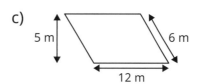

5 m

6 m

12 m

 m²

d)

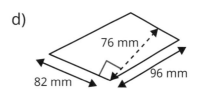

76 mm

96 mm

82 mm

 mm²

3   The triangle and rectangle have the same area.

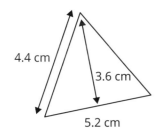

4.4 cm

3.6 cm

5.2 cm

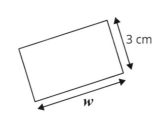

3 cm

w

Work out the width w of the rectangle. $w =$ [ ] cm

4   The area of a triangle is 36 cm²

The triangle has a base length of 9 cm.

What is the height of the triangle? height = [ ] cm

5   Find the area of each trapezium.

a)

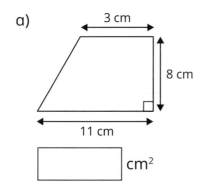

3 cm

8 cm

11 cm

 cm²

b)

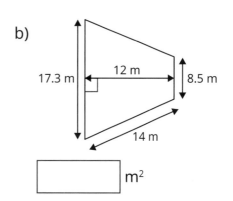

17.3 m

12 m

8.5 m

14 m

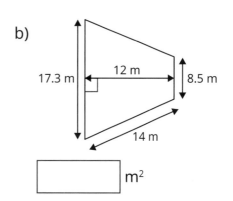 m²

99

6   The area of each trapezium is 42 cm². Find the missing lengths.

a)

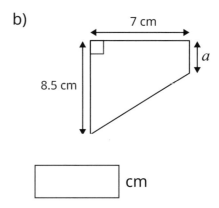

2 cm

h

10 cm

[ ] cm

b)

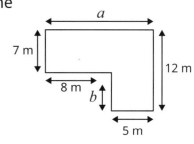

7 cm

a

8.5 cm

[ ] cm

7   a) Work out the unknown lengths a and b, and then find the perimeter of the shape.

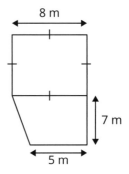

a

7 m

8 m

b

12 m

5 m

$a =$ [ ] m

$b =$ [ ] m

perimeter = [ ] m

b) Now work out the area of the shape.

area = [ ] m²

8   Find the area of the compound shape.

area = [ ] m²

8 m

7 m

5 m

9   What fraction of the shape is shaded?

Give your answer as a simplified fraction.

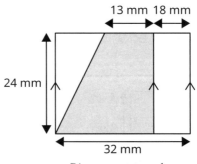

13 mm 18 mm

24 mm

32 mm

Diagram not to scale

How did you find these questions?

Very easy   1   2   3   4   5   6   7   8   9   10   Very difficult

Area of trapezia & circles

Date:

Let's remember

1. The base of a triangle is 13 cm.

   The perpendicular height is 6 cm.

   What is the area of the triangle? ⬚ cm²

2. What is the sum of the exterior angles of any polygon? ⬚ °

3. Complete the sentence.

   Co-interior angles sum to ⬚ °

4. Is the sequence 5, 9, 13, 17, … linear or non-linear? _____

Let's practise

1. Calculate the area of each circle. Give your answers in terms of π

   a)

   area = _____ m²

   b)

   area = _____ cm²

2   Find the area of each circle.

Give your answers in terms of π

a)

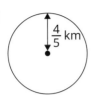

area = _____ km²

b)

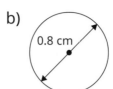

area = _____ cm²

3   Work out the area of each part of a circle.

Give your answers in terms of π

a)

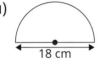

area = _____ cm²

b)

area = _____ mm²

4   Find the area of each circle.

Give your answers to 1 decimal place.

a)

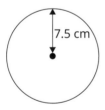

area = _____ cm²

b)

area = _____ m²

5   Work out the area of each part of a circle.

Give your answers to 3 significant figures.

a)

area = _____ cm²

b)

area = _____ m²

6   a) The area of a circle is 49π cm²

What is the radius of the circle? ☐ cm

b) The area of a circle is $\frac{25}{81}\pi$ m²

What is the diameter of the circle? $\frac{\boxed{}}{\boxed{}}$ m

c) The area of a semicircle is 128π mm².

What is the radius of the semicircle? ☐ mm

7   Work out the area of the shaded region in the shape.

Give your answer in terms of π _____ cm²

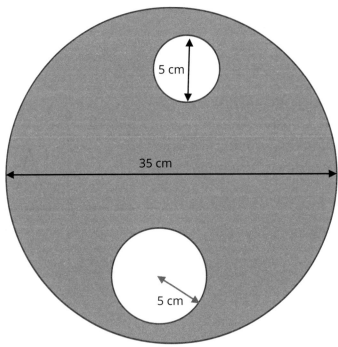

Diagram not to scale

8   Four circles are cut from a square piece of card as shown.

What area of the card is left? Give your answer to 2 d.p.

area = ☐ cm²

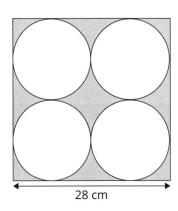

28 cm

How did you find these questions?

Very easy   1   2   3   4   5   6   7   8   9   10   Very difficult

Block 3 Line symmetry & reflection

In this block, you build on your knowledge of **line symmetry**. Here is half of a shape, with its **line of symmetry** drawn in. Can you tell what the name of the shape is?

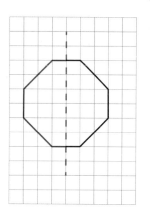

You look at the connection between line symmetry and **reflection**. You will need to use **square grids** for this work. If you reflect this shape in the **mirror line**, you get an isosceles triangle. Can you see why?

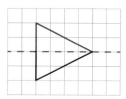

As well as square grids, you reflect shapes in **coordinate axes**. The mirror line doesn't always have to touch the shape. For example, you can use the **y-axis** as a mirror line for this triangle. Can you work out the coordinates of each vertex in the **image**?

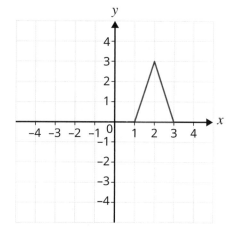

You also be reflect shapes in **diagonal** lines, like in this example. Thinking about the resulting shape, how many lines of symmetry will it have?

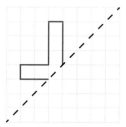

Key vocabulary

Line symmetry   Line of symmetry   Reflection   Mirror line

Square grid   Coordinate axes   *y*-axis   Object   Image   Diagonal

Line symmetry & reflection

Date:

Let's remember

1. The radius of a circle is 6 cm.

   What is the area of the circle?

   Give your answer in terms of π _____ cm

2. The area of a square is 144 cm²

   What is the side length of the square? ☐ cm

3. What is the sum of the interior angles of a hexagon? ☐ °

4. Expand $9(7a - 5)$ _____

Let's practise

1. Draw one line of symmetry on each shape.

   a)

   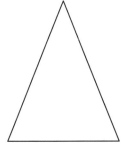

   b)

   c)

   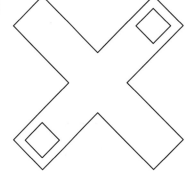

2   Here are some halves of shapes with their line of symmetry.
     Draw the rest of each shape.

a)

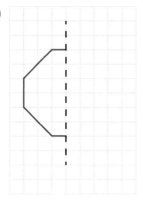

b)

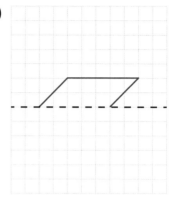

3   Reflect each shape in the given mirror line.

a)

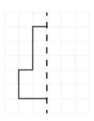

b)

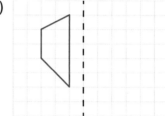

4   a) Reflect each shape in the *x*-axis.

i)

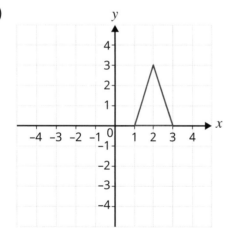

ii)

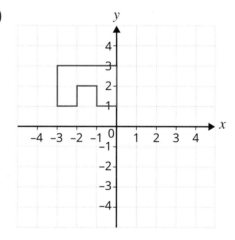

b) Reflect each shape in the *y*-axis.

i)

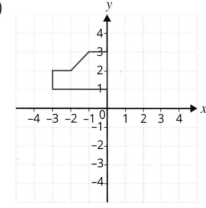

ii)

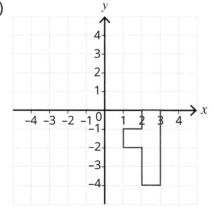

5   Reflect each shape in the given mirror line.

a)

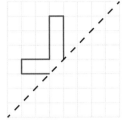

b)

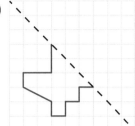

6   Two shapes are drawn on a coordinate grid.

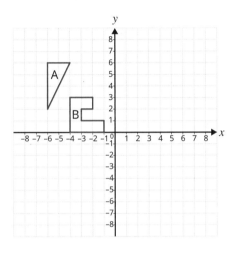

a) Reflect shape A in the line $x = -2$. Label your shape C.

Write the coordinates of the vertices of your new shape.

_____

b) Reflect shape B in the line $y = x$. Label your shape D.

c) Plot the points (–5, –2), (–7, –2), (–7, –5) and (–5, –4) and join them to form a trapezium.

d) Reflect the trapezium from part c) in the y-axis.

7   Here are the coordinates of four points.

W (–7, 0)   X (–3, 5)   Y (1, 5)   Z (–3, 0)

a) What shape is WXYZ? _____

b) WXYZ is reflected in the line $y = -2$

Write the coordinates of the vertices of the reflected shape.

_____

Block 4 The data handling cycle

In this block, you revisit **statistics,** and put it all together into the **data handling cycle**. That is just a way of describing what you do when you conduct a **statistical enquiry**. You explore **questionnaires** that are used to **collect data,** like this one. Can you think of anything wrong with this question?

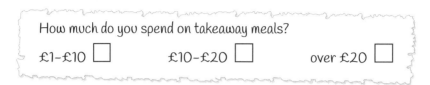

How much do you spend on takeaway meals?

£1–£10 ☐   £10–£20 ☐   over £20 ☐

You **organise data** into a **frequency table**, like this one that shows the number of different coloured sweets in a packet of sweets. The table clearly shows that green sweets occur most often.

Colour	Red	Blue	Green	Orange
Frequency	10	12	15	13

You also **compare** data given in different data sets. This **line graph** shows sales in two different ice cream parlours over a 12-month period. What is the same and what is different about the sales in the two shops?

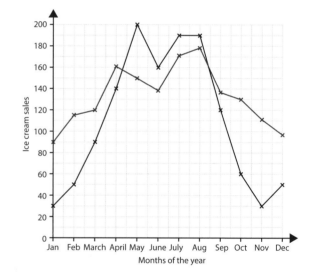

You will **criticise** the way that data is **represented** in diagrams. This **bar chart** shows the results of some students who were asked if they like English or Maths best. Can you see why the graph might be **misleading**?

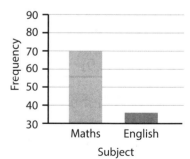

Key vocabulary

Statistics   Data handling cycle   Statistical enquiry   Questionnaire

Collect data   Organise data   Frequency table   Compare   Criticise   Represent

Interpret   Misleading   Range   Pictogram   Bar chart   Pie chart   Mean

The data handling cycle

Date:

Let's remember

1   How many lines of symmetry does a square have? ☐

2   A circle has diameter 6 cm.

What is the area of the circle?

Give your answer in terms of π _____ cm^2

3   What is the size of each interior angle in a regular hexagon? ☐ °

4   Write 0.83 as a percentage. ☐

Let's practise

1   Mo asks students in his class what their favourite safari animals are.

a) Complete the data collection chart.

Animal	Tally	Frequency
Lion	ⵜⵜⵜⵜ ||	
Monkey		6
Elephant	ⵜⵜⵜⵜ |||	
Zebra		2
Leopard	ⵜⵜⵜⵜ ⵜⵜⵜⵜ |	
Other		1
	Total	

b) Which animal is the most popular? _____

2   Ron writes this question to investigate how long students spend completing their homework.

> How long do you spend on your homework?
>
> 0 – 10 minutes ☐   10 – 30 minutes ☐   30 – 45 minutes ☐   1 hour ☐

a) Write two things that are wrong with this question.

_____

_____

b) Design a better question for Ron's questionnaire.

_____

_____

3   The pictogram shows information about the number of chocolate bars sold by a shop on Monday, Tuesday and Wednesday in a certain week.

Monday   ◯ ◯

Tuesday   ◯ ◖   Key:

Wednesday ◯ ◯ ◺   ◯ represents
                     4 chocolate
Thursday   bars

Friday

a) Write the number of chocolate bars sold on

   i) Monday ☐   ii) Tuesday ☐   iii) Wednesday ☐

b) 15 chocolate bars were sold on Thursday.

   The number of chocolate bars sold on Friday was double the number of chocolate bars sold on Wednesday.

   Use this information to complete the pictogram.

4   There are 30 students in a class. Each day, the students can receive one achievement point. The chart shows the number of achievement points that the class receive each day.

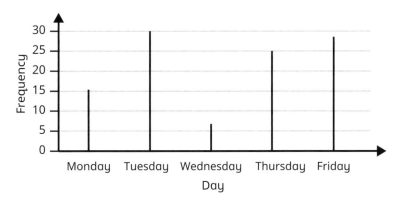

a) On which day did all the students get an achievement point? _____

b) How many achievement points were received on Wednesday?

c) How many achievement points were received in total for the week?

d) What is the mean number of achievement points received each day?

5   All of the Year 8 students in a school were asked their favourite subject out of Maths, English and Science. Here is a bar chart showing the results.

85 students chose science as their favourite subject.

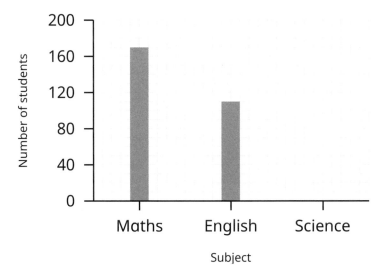

a) Complete the bar chart to show this information.

b) How many more students chose maths than chose English?

How did you find these questions?

Very easy   1   2   3   4   5   6   7   8   9   10   Very difficult

The data handling cycle

Date:

Let's remember

1   Identify two things that are wrong with this question.

> How many times do you go to the supermarket?
>
> 1 – 5 ☐   5 – 10 ☐   more than 10 ☐

2   How many lines of symmetry does an equilateral triangle have? ☐

3   A rectangle has length 8 cm and width 3 cm.

What is the area of the rectangle? ☐ cm²

4   Write the decimal multiplier that you would use to decrease a number by 35%

☐

Let's practise

1   Some students in Year 7 and Year 8 were asked how about their favourite pizza.
The bar chart gives information about the results.

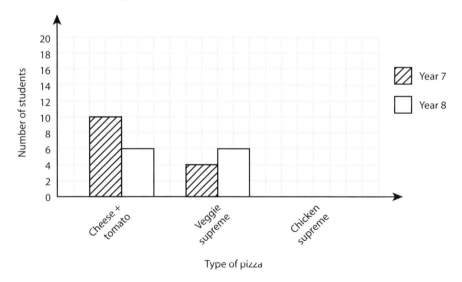

a) How many Year 7 students chose cheese and tomato? ☐

b) How many Year 8 students chose veggie supreme? ☐

c) 16 Year 7 students chose chicken supreme.

17 Year 8 students chose chicken supreme.

Show this information on the bar chart.

2 Some people were asked to choose their favourite chocolate.

Favourite chocolate

a) What percentage of people chose dark chocolate as their favourite?

b) What fraction of people chose white chocolate as their favourite? Give your answer in its simplest form.

c) What is the angle in the pie chart for milk chocolate? _____

3 Some students were asked their favourite sport out of football, rugby and tennis. The table shows the results for females and males.

	Football	Rugby	Tennis
Year 10	30	5	25
Year 11	38	17	5

Draw a dual bar chart to represent this data.

Class 1   Class 2

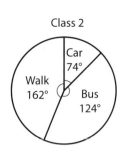

4   Students in Class 1 and Class 2 say how they get to school. The pie charts show the results.

5 students travel by car in Class 1

a) How many students take the bus in Class 1?

_____

b) Eva says, "The pie charts show that more students walk in Class 2"

Is Eva correct? _____

Explain your answer.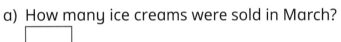

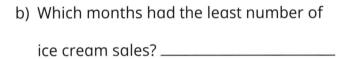

5   The line graph shows the number of ice cream sales in a shop over a 12-month period.

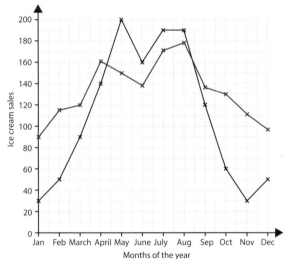

a) How many ice creams were sold in March?

b) Which months had the least number of

ice cream sales? _____

c) Which month had the greatest number of

ice cream sales? _____

d) Between which two months was the biggest change in the number of ice creams sold?

_____

e) Is it possible to use the graph to tell how many ice creams were sold on 1st October? Why?

_____

How did you find these questions?

Very easy   1   2   3   4   5   6   7   8   9   10   Very difficult

The data handling cycle

Date:

Let's remember

1. What is the total of the angles in a pie chart? ☐ °

2. Design a question to find out how often people go to the supermarket.

   _____

   _____

   _____

3. A circle has diameter 10 cm.

   What is the area of the circle? Give you answer in terms of π

   _____ cm²

4. Work out 12% of £5000

   £ ☐

Let's practise

1. Some students are asked their favourite subject at school. The subjects are labelled from A to H. The results are shown on the pie chart and the bar chart.

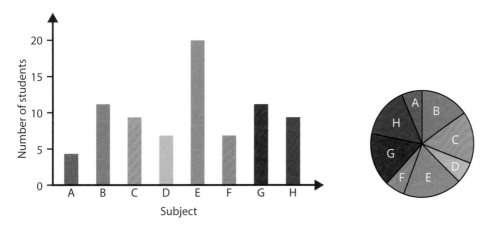

Which do you think is the more useful representation of the data? Why?

   _____

   _____

115

2   Which type of diagram would you use to represent the data in each of the tables?

a)

Colour	Red	Blue	Green	Orange
Frequency	10	12	15	13

Type of diagram _____

Reason _____

b)

Colour	Red	Blue	Green	Orange
Frequency	1	12	35	8

Type of diagram _____

Reason _____

c)

Time	5 pm	6 pm	7 pm	8 pm
Frequency	54	78	96	43

Type of diagram _____

Reason _____

3   Kim records the ages of 40 people at a party.

19 42 51 67 46 22 42 26 48 14 32 24 43 55 11 55 62 63 22 47

14 26 13 47 12 53 28 68 21 37 52 25 11 64 21 55 22 66 51 26

a) Complete the table to show the information.

Age	Tally	Frequency
10–20		
21–30		
31–40		
41–50		
51–60		
61–70		

b) Use the table to work out how many people are 41 years of age or over. [ ]

c) How many people are 50 or under? [ ]

4   50 students take a maths test. The percentage scores are shown in the table.

Percentage score (s)	Frequency
$0 < s \leq 20$	3
$20 < s \leq 40$	7
$40 < s \leq 60$	14
$60 < s \leq 80$	19
$80 < s \leq 100$	7

a) How many students scored more than 60%? ☐

b) Can you tell exactly how many students scored 40%? _____

    Explain your answer.

    _____

    _____

c) Estimate the number of students who scored less than 50%. ☐

5   Find the range of each set of data.

a) 38 cm, 29 cm, 62 cm, 51 cm _____

b) 3.4 kg, 5.2 kg, 2.5 kg, 7.2 kg, 1.8 kg _____

6   The range of some numbers is 48

The greatest number is 102

What is the lowest value? ☐

7   Find the range of the lengths.

35 mm, 9 cm, 16 cm

_____

How did you find these questions?

Very easy   1   2   3   4   5   6   7   8   9   10   Very difficult

The data handling cycle

Date:

Let's remember

1 A group of people were asked for their favourite colour.

Colour	Red	Blue	Yellow	Green	Orange
Frequency	10	5	1	8	2

What fraction of the people said green was their favourite colour?

2 A group of people were asked to choose their favourite colour.

What fraction of people chose yellow as their favourite?

Give your answer in its simplest form.

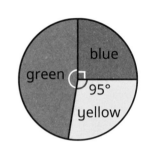

3 How many lines of symmetry does a regular pentagon have?

4 Write 10^6 as an ordinary number.

Let's practise

1 The bar chart shows the number of dogs and cats owned by students in each year group.

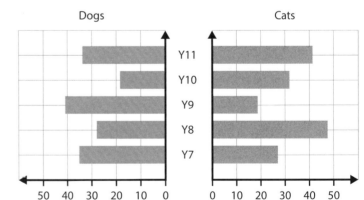

a) How many dogs are owned by Year 9 students?

b) Are more dogs or cats owned by students in Year 11? _____

c) How many more cats than dogs are owned by students in Year 10?

2   Two groups of people were asked if they prefer tea or coffee.

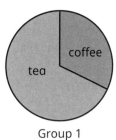

The pie charts show the results.

Explain what the pie charts show.

Group 1   Group 2

_____

_____

3   The chart shows the number of books an author sells in two different bookshops.

Shop A   Shop B

Key: 📖 = 100 books

a) How many books were sold in

   i)   Shop A in January? [   ]

   ii) Shop B in April? [   ]

   iii) Shop A in February? [   ]

b) What is similar about the number of books sold at the two shops between January and June?

_____

_____

c) What is different about the number of books sold at the two shops between January and June?

_____

_____

4   Some students are asked if they like English or Maths best.

The results are shown in a bar chart.

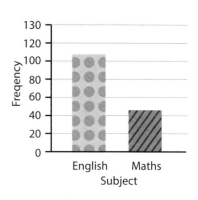

a) Is a bar chart the best way of representing this information? Explain your answer.

_____

_____

b) Some other students are asked if they prefer English or Maths. The results are shown in a bar chart.

Why might the graph be misleading?

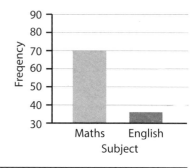

_____

_____

_____

5   A company advertises a packet of biscuits that contains 25% extra free.

Explain why this advertisement could be seen as misleading.

_____

_____

6   The pictogram shows the number of ice creams sold in a day.

Criticise the chart.

_____

_____

_____

Ice cream sales		
Vanilla	🍦🍦🍦🍦🍦	53
Chocolate	🍦🍦🍦🍦	42
Strawberry	🍦🍦🍦	39
Mint	🍦	14

How did you find these questions?

Very easy   1   2   3   4   5   6   7   8   9   10   Very difficult

Block 5 Measures of location

In this block, you learn about **averages**, or **measures of location**. You have already learned a bit about the **mean** and the **median**, but here you are introduced to another kind of average, called the **mode**. The mode is the most common value. These six numbers have a mode of 28, a mean of 35 and a median of 35

You work out the mean, median and mode of data given in a **frequency table**, like this one. This is **discrete** data, because you can't have $1\frac{1}{2}$ televisions!

Number of televisions	0	1	2	3	4
Frequency	7	46	95	123	167

You also identify **outliers.** There are two outliers in this **scatter graph** – can you see them?

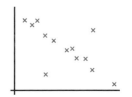

You also learn how to **estimate** the mean of **grouped data**, like in this table that shows the time it takes students to get to school. You have to use the **midpoint** of each **class** in our calculations. It is only an estimate because you do not know the exact times.

Time (t minutes)	Frequency	Midpoint	Frequency × midpoint
$0 \le t < 10$	3	5	15
$10 \le t < 20$	7	15	105
$20 \le t < 30$	14		

You will compare data sets using averages and the **range.** The table shows the mean and range for the weights of two breeds of dog. What can you say about Breed A compared to Breed B?

	Breed A	Breed B
Mean	33 kg	31 kg
Range	7 kg	4 kg

Key vocabulary

Average   Measure of location   Mean   Median   Mode   Frequency table

Discrete   Continuous   Outlier   Scatter graph   Estimate

Grouped data   Midpoint   Class   Range

Measures of location

Date:

Let's remember

1. A pie chart is split into 5 equal sectors.

   What is the angle of each sector? [ ] °

2. The masses of some chimpanzees are shown in the table.

Mass (kg)	$0 < t \leq 50$	$50 < t \leq 100$	$100 < t \leq 150$
Frequency	26	48	19

   How many chimpanzees have a mass greater than 50 kg? [ ]

3. If ◯ = 8 chimpanzees what do ◯◯◯◯ ? represent? [ ]

4. Write 6 600 000 in standard form. _____

Let's practise

1. Find the mean, median and mode of each set of data.

   a) 8, 7, 8, 8, 4

      Mean: _____

      Median: _____

      Mode: _____

   b) 6, 11, 3, 7

      Mean: _____

      Median: _____

      Mode: _____

   c) 29, 37, 55, 29, 55, 41

      Mean: _____

      Median: _____

      Mode: _____

2   Here are the number of football goals scored by a football team in five home games
and four away games.

Home games: 3, 1, 2, 2, 1

Away games: 4, 4, 1, 0

a) Write the modal number of goals scored in all of the games. ▢

b) Work out the median number of goals scored in the away games. ▢

c) Work out the range of the number of goals scored in home games. ▢

d) Work out the mean of all the goals scored. ▢

e) Another away game was played, and the football team scored four goals.

Without further calculations, explain how this will affect the

i)   mean number of goals scored in all of the games

_____

_____

_____

ii) mode number of goals scored in all of the games

_____

_____

_____

3 Six numbers have a mode of 28, a mean of 35 and a median of 35

a) Fill in the cards to show what the numbers could be.

b) Work out the range of your set of numbers.

c) Is there another choice of numbers that you could have made for the cards in part a? How would this affect your answer to part b)?

_____

_____

4 The mean of nine numbers is 37

Five of the numbers have a mean of 42

What is the mean of the other four numbers?

5 Viewers give a star rating, from 1 to 5, for new films at the cinema.
The star rating of a new film is shown in the table.

H

Star rating	Frequency
1	5
2	18
3	26
4	
5	16

The mean star rating of the film is 3.39

Calculate the value of the missing frequency.

How did you find these questions?

| Very easy | 1 | 2 | 3 | 4 | 5 | 6 | 7 | 8 | 9 | 10 | Very difficult |

Measures of location

Date:

Let's remember

1 Find the mean of the set of data.

5   6   8   9   2

mean = ▢

2 A local election campaign features this advert.

Why is this graph misleading?

_____

_____

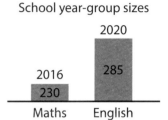

School year-group sizes

3 A circle has radius 16.2 cm.

What is the diameter of the circle? _____ cm

4 Mrs Dean's shopping bill totals £41.86

She gives the shop assistant £50.

How much change will she receive?

£ ▢

Let's practise

1 a) Here are the masses, in kilograms, of some dogs.

15   21   38   11   89   10   13   32

Which of the values is an outlier? _____

b) Explain what is meant by the term 'outlier'.

_____

_____

125

2   The table shows the mean and range of points scored per basketball match by two teams.

	Mean	Range
Team A	27	25
Team B	31	14

a) On average, which team scored more points per game? How do you know?

_____

b) Which team is more consistent? How do you know?

_____

3   Write the midpoints of the class intervals.

a) $0 \leq x < 20$ ☐

b) $1 \leq x < 20$ ☐

c) $20 \leq x < 30$ ☐

d) $21 \leq x < 30$ ☐

e) $30 \leq x < 50$ ☐

f) $31 \leq x < 50$ ☐

4   Ron asked students in his class how long it takes them to get to school.

H

Time (t minutes)	Frequency	Midpoint	Frequency × midpoint
$0 \leq t < 10$	3		
$10 \leq t < 20$	7		
$20 \leq t < 30$	14		
$30 \leq t < 40$	4		
$40 \leq t < 50$	2		
$50 \leq t < 60$	1		
Total			

a) How many students did Ron ask? ☐

b) Complete the calculation to find an estimate of the mean time for students to get to school.

$$\text{estimate of mean} \approx \frac{\text{total time}}{\text{total frequency}} = \frac{\boxed{}}{\boxed{}} = \boxed{} \text{ minutes}$$

5 The table shows information about the price of some books.

Cost (c pounds)	Frequency	Midpoint	Frequency × midpoint
$0 < c \leq 3$	25		
$3 < c \leq 5$	17		
$5 < c \leq 7$	32		
$7 < c \leq 10$	11		

a) Complete the empty columns of the table.

b) Work out an estimate for the mean price of the books.

£ _____

c) Mo works out the mean to be £8.50

Explain, without doing any calculations, how Mo is incorrect.

_____

_____

d) Write the modal class of the books. _____

6 The table shows the duration of some films.

Duration (d hours)	Frequency	Midpoint	Frequency × midpoint
$0 < d \leq 0.5$	2		
$0.5 < d \leq 1$			3
	18	1.5	
	12		27
	10	2.75	27.5

a) Fill in any missing information in the table.

b) Write the modal class of duration. _____

c) Work out an estimate for the mean duration. _____ hours

How did you find these questions?

Very easy   1   2   3   4   5   6   7   8   9   10   Very difficult

Summer term   Self-assessment

Time to reflect

Look back through the work you have done this term. Think about what you enjoyed and what you found easy or hard. Talk about this to your teacher and someone at home.

Try these questions	How do you feel about this topic? Tick the box.
The diagram shows a regular decagon. Work out the size of the angle x. $x =$ [ ] ° If you need a reminder, look back at angles in parallel lines & polygons on pages 87–96	☐ I am confident and could teach someone else. ☐ I think I understand but I need practice. ☐ I don't understand and need help.
A circle of radius 8 cm has two identical circles inside it as shown. Calculate the area of the shaded region, giving your answer to 1 decimal place. shaded area = [ ] cm^2 If you need a reminder, look back at the area of trapezia & circles on pages 97–103	☐ I am confident and could teach someone else. ☐ I think I understand but I need practice. ☐ I don't understand and need help.
The pie charts show the favourite subject of 180 students in Year 7 and some students in Year 11 a) How many chose Science in Year 7? [ ] b) 120 students chose maths in Year 11. Gabriel says that slightly more students chose English in Year 7 than in Year 11. Is he correct? Show your reasoning. _____ _____ If you need a reminder, look back at the data handling cycle on pages 108–120	☐ I am confident and could teach someone else. ☐ I think I understand but I need practice. ☐ I don't understand and need help.

Year 7: Maths 130°, English 110°, Science

Year 11: Maths 200°, English, Science